G000256313

BRIERLEY HILL

ROUND OAK, HARTS HILL, LEVEL STREET, MERRY HILL, QUARRY BANK, MILL STREET, THE DELPH, SILVER END & HAWBUSH

NED WILLIAMS & THE MOUNT PLEASANT LOCAL HISTORY GROUP

The History Press

THE MOUNT PLEASANT LOCAL HISTORY GROUP

Janet & Geoff Attwood, Marie Billingham, Mary Brookes, Carol Cobb, Kath & Ken Day, Derek & Margaret Homer, Jack Hill, John James, Lynda Laker, Peter & Jo Lloyd, Sheila Marshall, Carol Parsons, Joan Pearson, Norma Pearson, Mike Perkins, Margaret Priest, Doreen Rutter, Dennis Rydes, Margaret Slater, Susan Webb.

Front cover photograph: Brierley Hill has an excellent market – seen here in about 1940. It was opened on Saturday 20 December 1930 on a day when Brierley Hill Alliance was playing 'at home'! An open air market had existed on the site since at least the 1880s, but a Nottingham-based company purchased the site and they asked local architects Jennings & Homer to design a new covered market hall. It was built by Messrs Batham & Beddall using steelwork prefabricated locally by Messrs Hill & Smith of Canal Street, Harts Hill. While it was being built market stall-holders carried on their trade on the wakes ground at the end of Cottage Street. *(Roy Pugh)*

Back cover photograph: A view from Pedmore Road back up The Levels.

Title page photograph: Samuel Massey and his wife Elizabeth stand by the doorway of their shop at Round Oak in about 1912. Sam (1863–1962) ran a grocery business, and bakery and even sold cattle and livestock feed. His baker stands between Elizabeth and another employee, while someone else prepares to take out the delivery cart (see page 36). *(Graham Beckley Collection)*

There are persons still living who remember Brierley Hill, and all the district all around, as an extensive forest; but the opening of the mines has completely altered the face of the country, for it is now a forest of houses.

Kelly's Directory of 1845

First published 2011
Reprinted 2011

The History Press
The Mill, Brimscombe Port
Stroud, Gloucestershire, GL5 2QG
www.thehistorypress.co.uk

British Library Cataloguing in Publication Data.
A catalogue record for this book is available from the British Library.

isbn 978 0 7524 5995 0

Typesetting and origination by The History Press
Printed in Great Britain

CONTENTS

Introduction   5

1.   Brierley Hill Town Centre   7

2.   Round Oak including The Wallows   35

3.   Harts Hill   47

4.   Level Street & Merry Hill   53

5.   Quarry Bank   59

6.   Mill Street to Quarry Bank   73

7.   Down to The Delph   87

8.   Silver End, Brettell Lane & Hawbush   95

9.   Brierley Hill Folk   119

Acknowledgements   128

ARMORIAL BEARINGS: BRIERLEY HILL, STAFFS

SINE · LABORE NIHIL · FLORET

THE ARMS WHICH WERE ASSIGNED TO THE COUNCIL BY LETTERS PATENT 19 JUNE 1942 combine representations of the local industries and the arms of Kingswinford. The glass, iron & steel, and the fire clay industries are denoted by the beacons. The boars' heads are the 'King's Swine' and the two circles in the centre across which run wavy lines represent the fords adjoining the ancient manor by which swine crossed the manor to the waste lands beyond. The rose represents the briar which used to abound around the Hill and from which the town gets its name. The knot is the Stafford knot: the motto means 'Without labour nothing flourishes.' (WRITTEN AND RUBRICATED AT THE SCHOOL OF ART · BRIERLEY HILL · IN THE COUNTY OF STAFFORD · BY H W WOODWARD · 1958)

This particular document featuring the Brierley Hill coat of arms is the work of Bill Woodward who was the town's chief librarian from 1938 until his retirement. He was born in Grimsby in 1913, and was therefore only twenty-four when appointed to the job in Brierley Hill. After the Second World War he forged ahead with his library work, and began to build up a glass collection – the basis of the current collection at Broadfield House. He supported the study of local history, the local art society, and numerous literary societies. He died on 11 August 1999.

INTRODUCTION

Our first book about Brierley Hill explored the western end of the town centre from St Michael's Church up to the Five Ways, and then traversed the villages of Brockmoor, Bromley and Pensnett. This second volume has to carry out the huge task of continuing our journey through the town centre, not only along the High Street, but also in many side streets, and out towards Round Oak. We then need to continue our circumnavigation of Brierley Hill's satellites, coming back across The Wallows which also brings us to Round Oak, and out to Harts Hill. We then have to descend The Levels (i.e. Level Street) and cross that no-man's land that has become the Merry Hill Retail Complex to reach Quarry Bank. From Quarry Bank we can make our way back to the town centre via Mill Street, or plunge down into The Delph to take us on to Silver End and, ultimately, to Hawbush.

All these areas have their own distinct identity, history and loyalties on the part of the inhabitants, but it is remarkable how they all have interacted in the process of being Brierley Hill. On the next page we meet Ann Stansfield while working as headmistress of Brockmoor Secondary girls school, but she is equally well known as the head of the Pensnett school as seen in the previous book (*Brierley Hill: Brockmoor, Bromley & Pensnett in Old Photographs*, page 123). Among her staff is the school secretary, Mary Rousell, who had also attended the school as a pupil. Mary has links with many other parts of Brierley Hill, particularly Quarry Bank. Also in the second row is Gloria Smart who had links with Harts Hill and Silver End, and so we could go on. . .

Thus the study of any one part of Brierley Hill introduces connections with another, and of course this volume includes the mighty Round Oak Steel Works – a huge enterprise which drew workers from all over Brierley Hill and far beyond.

In this way Brierley Hill has been a microcosm of the Black Country – a region in which people could fiercely identify with the 'patch' they lived in but also inhabit a vast network of criss-crossing lives in which everyone crossed each other's patch in search of education, work, shopping, leisure, social or sporting activity. If this seems a complex matter to try to understand, it is dwarfed by the task of trying to provide an account of how the area has changed. This book also has to reflect the way in which a thriving industrial town has had to settle for being a neighbour to a major modern retailing phenomenon, which it can neither ignore nor embrace. At the same time we have to contemplate the old Brierley Hill of sausages and steel – a large progressive urban district, once part of the county of Stafford, and forever a part of the Black Country.

We hope readers will also look at our first book on Brierley Hill, and our previous books on Quarry Bank, one of which includes a large section on The Delph. Readers should also go back to Stan Hill's two books: *Brierley Hill in Old Photographs* and *Stan Hill's Brierley Hill And Life*.

Since the production of our first book about Brierley Hill it was perhaps inevitable that other pictures relevant to the areas covered in that book would come to light. This postcard view of Brockmoor school is one such example. The council houses in the background built at the end of the 1940s provided new homes for people displaced by slum clearance in areas like Level Street – covered in this volume. *(Maureen Dean)*

Staff and fifth form at Brookmoor Secondary Girls School in 1969. (The following year they were amalgamated with the lads from Mill Street who, in turn, had come from Bent Street.) As mentioned on the previous page, Miss Stansfield, seen in the centre of the front row, later had to unite this school with the one in Pensnett. Mary Rousell, school secretary and ex-pupil, is second from left in the second row. Mary, who supplied this picture, reappears on page 24 of our book *Quarry Bank & The Delph*.

1

BRIERLEY HILL
TOWN CENTRE

O ur task in the next few pages is to continue our west to east transect of central Brierley Hill begun in *Brierley Hill: Brockmoor, Bromley & Pensnett in Old Photographs*. We start at the Five Ways. Up until the 1960s the Town Arms occupied the corner of Cottage Street and High Street but now the Walter Smith shop (formerly Marsh & Baxter's) is our obvious starting point. However, before progressing eastwards we will explore the area penetrated by Moor Street, where we find the old Library and Art College and the mysteries of Fenton Street and Albion Street.

Returning to the High Street, we will continue our journey with a glimpse of Chattin & Horton's fine store – a reminder that the High Street once had a 'penny side' and 'sixpenny side'. The former was home to shops like the Penny Bazaar, and the latter was home to Chattin & Horton's. Perhaps the arrival of the covered market on the sixpenny side ended this demarcation.

Beyond the crossroads by the Civic Centre we have to continue along Dudley Road as well as explore Bank Street, Bent Street and John Street.

When this picture was taken in December 1959 the High Street could still boast a small Woolworths and a branch of Timothy White, as well as the elegant tiled frontage of Southan Brothers' menswear shop. *(Stuart Perry/Express & Star)*

The Marsh & Baxter shop used to stand on this prominent High Street position close to the Five Ways (opposite Moor Street), the business having moved from its original shop which was opposite the police station. These premises had previously been occupied by George Mason's. *(NW)*

Staff line up in the entrance to the ex-Marsh & Baxter shop in Brierley Hill, owned by Walter Smith, a Birmingham-based butcher, since the 1980s. This picture was taken in March 1984. *(NW)*

Moor Street, 1970, looking up to the Five Ways. The cake shop seems empty but Wilkinson's cycle shop, followed by Higgs, the butcher, both still seem to be in business. *(John James)*

In October 1985 these shops at the top of Moor Street seemed to be struggling to survive. Moor Street Fish & Chips was more than just a shop – it was a 'Fish Restaurant & Café'. The shop has survived, but not the enamel sign. Its neighbour was already empty, then came an antiques shop that had once been the bicycle shop, and then an upholsterer. These shops have been demolished. *(NW)*

Brierley Hill's elegant library and 'Adult School' in Moor Street. It was built during 1903/4 to the designs of J. Lewis Harper, the Urban District Council's Surveyor. After the library services moved to new premises in the High Street the building was 'reinvented' as the International Glass Centre, eventually coming under the control of Dudley College. With the decline of the local glass industry the number of students studying glass design and manufacture has also declined and Dudley College announced its intention to close the facility, shutting it down in the summer of 2009. *(Workman Collection)*

Fenton Street divides from Moor Street, and was home to the Fenton Street Mission Hall, photographed here in 1966. The original 'Gospel Union Tabernacle' on this site was a wooden shed but Enoch Harris built this replacement 'with his own hands', and it opened on 7 June 1896. It was modernised in 1966 but was compulsorily purchased by the council and was then demolished. The congregation then moved to a new building in William Street. *(Stan Hill Collection)*

The first turning off Moor Street is Albion Street, and close to the junction is this preserved Iron & Steel Warehouse. It was probably designed by Messrs Rollinson & Beckley in the 1870s and built for Messrs Wise & Longland. Edward John Wise was an ironmonger based in the High Street who appears to have gone into partnership with a fellow High Street retailer: Henry Longland. *(NW)*

This interesting house was built as their own home by the Bishop brothers, local builders who built the Edwardian houses of Adelaide Street, etc. It was demolished in the 1980s and the site now houses the local headquarters of the Samaritans. *(NW)*

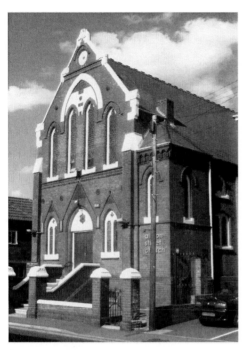

Dissent and non-conformity have both been strong in Greater Brierley Hill, possibly first represented by the Pensnett Meeting House built in the place we now know as Cradley Forge in 1704 – over fifty years before the Church of England started to plan St Michael's Church. Independent dissenters who took the name 'Congregationalists' seem to have a presence in Brierley Hill going back to the beginning of the nineteenth century. At one time they met at Harts Hill and then Mill Street before coming to Albion Street in 1875. The building seen here was opened on 6 December 1882. The church became 'United Reform' in 1973, but the congregation was in decline and the church closed in 1976, some members transferring to Bank Street. *(NW)*

The old Congregationalist church in Albion Street was sold to a Fellowship of the Assemblies of God that had been meeting in the chapel in Seagers Lane, under the pastorship of Cyril Baker (left). They opened at Albion Street on 30 April 1977, and Cyril's son, David Baker (right), became the new pastor, photographed in 2008. *(NW)*

Resuming our journey along Brierley Hill High Street, next door to Marsh & Baxter's shop was Chattin & Horton – a household drapery, furnishing and clothing business started in 1910 by Joseph Chattin and George Horton. It grew and survived long enough to be run by the third generation of Chattins, but closed on 20 March 1976, shortly after this photograph was taken. *(John James)*

A Lily White postcard of the High Street seen in the 1930s, looking towards Dudley from within a few yards of the Five Ways. The Dudley–Stourbridge electric trams had replaced the steam trams in late 1900, only to be replaced by Midland Red buses on 1 March 1930 – hence the absence of track, wires and poles. *(Michael Reuter)*

This building, photographed in July 2001, was once the brand new premises of the Brierley Hill Branch of the Dudley Co-operative Society. It was opened by Alderman John Molyneux, the society's President, on 24 January 1959 and was designed by Messrs Webb and Gray, and built by Fletcher's, both local firms. It was built on the site of an old furniture store and from then on a number of trading activities (grocery, butchery, drapery, electrical and hardware, etc.) could be brought together under one roof. These had previously been provided in separate Co-operative shops in Brierley Hill. The Co-op closed the store in the early 1980s. (NW)

The Market Hall was built at the beginning of the 1930s and was designed by Messrs Jennings and Homer, local architects. It actually opened on 20 December 1930, using the table-like stalls seen here. Well-known marketeers include Ann Marsh, Geoff Brown, Walter James, Mollie Bastock, Alf Hodgkiss, Evelyn Howells, Ernie Capewell and Leslie Cox. (Roy Pugh)

Above: Jones Brothers' radio and TV shop at 153 High Street, photographed in June 1982. The four shops in this block once belonged to Drinkwater's, the drapers also associated with Wednesbury. Don and Hartley Jones bought the premises from them in the mid-1930s. By the 1980s it was being run by Hartley's son, Michael Jones, who maintained the shops' clock, quality sign-writing and glass window signs. *(NW)*

Right: A.C. Kendrick's corn shop at 159 High Street, photographed in November 1985. Kendrick's operated similar stores in Blackheath and Old Hill (Reddal Hill). This was a typical late Victorian shop-front with its side entrance with porch, its simple columns and pilasters and windows with quarter-lights. *(NW)*

The Misses L. and A. Nicholson ran a ladies' and children's wear store at 161 Brierley Hill High Street, in a distinctive two-storey shop. The arched windows, designed to let the maximum amount of daylight into the upstairs showroom, make the building immediately recognisable today. This picture was probably taken in the 1920s. The Odeon cinema was opposite this shop. *(Author's Collection)*

The same shop can be readily identified in this 2009 picture of this section of the High Street, photographed from the corner of Pearson Street. *(NW)*

Brierley Hill Town Hall, first built in 1874 as a public hall, at a cost of £3,000. It provided accommodation for the council when the UDC was formed in 1894 but ten years later the Moor Street building provided an alternative. It was also home to the town's first library which opened in 1875, and the main public hall was first used for film and theatrical entertainment by R. Colin in 1910 as the Tivoli, but was better known after 1912 as the Queens Hall, when leased as a cinema by Pooles' Perfect Pictures. They passed the lease on to Cecil Couper, their manager, and he ran it until the lease expired in 1939. It became increasingly dilapidated during and after the Second World War and was eventually demolished in 1968. *(Ron and Madge Workman Collection)*

Brierley Hill's Odeon opened as the Picture House on 1 October 1928, and closed on 25 July 1959. The site of the Odeon was then used by Fine Fare – the town's first supermarket. *(John Maltby)*

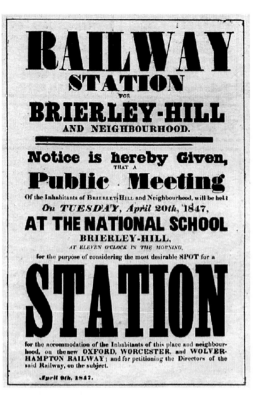

RAILWAY STATION
FOR
BRIERLEY-HILL
AND NEIGHBOURHOOD.

Notice is hereby Given,
THAT A
Public Meeting
Of the Inhabitants of BRIERLEY HILL and Neighbourhood, will be held

On TUESDAY, April 20th, 1847,
AT THE NATIONAL SCHOOL
BRIERLEY-HILL,
AT ELEVEN O'CLOCK IN THE MORNING,
for the purpose of considering the most desirable SPOT for a

STATION

for the accommodation of the Inhabitants of this place and neighbourhood, on the new OXFORD, WORCESTER, and WOLVERHAMPTON RAILWAY; and for petitioning the Directors of the said Railway, on the subject.

April 9th, 1847.

Before taking in the last section of the High Street and reaching the junction with Bank Street and Level Street, let's take a detour to the station and the little network of streets built between the railway and the High Street – an area of Edwardian 'artisan dwellings' built by the Bishop brothers. When the Oxford, Worcester & Wolverhampton Railway opened between Stourbridge Junction and Dudley at the end of 1852, the local station was provided at Round Oak – perhaps as a result of views expressed at the meeting advertised on the right. The station built at the bottom of Fenton Street – almost in Brockmoor – was added on 1 December 1858. A siding just north of the station provided access to a platform used for despatching parcels of Marsh & Baxter's products.

West End, later known as Bradleymoor Road, is a cul-de-sac off the junction of Fenton Street and Station Road, and was part of the Edwardian development of this area of Brierley Hill, overlooking the railway line. The station was on the embankment seen in the right background of the picture, but had long since closed when this picture was taken in the 1980s. *(Stan Hill Collection)*

Class 51xx 2–6–2T no. 4179 coasts into Brierley Hill station on 21 August 1961 with a train from Worcester to Wolverhampton. Kingswinford Junction North signal-box can be seen in the distance and the Moor Lane ('Tackeroo') bridge beyond. The row of houses behind the box have been demolished but the large double-fronted house facing the railway still exists. Passenger trains ceased the following summer (1962) but freight trains still use this line today. *(Michael Mensing)*

The top picture was probably taken from this footbridge, but this 1958 view is looking in the opposite direction (i.e. towards Dudley) and shows 2–6–2T no. 5151 with a stopping train from Wolverhampton. Note the pigeon baskets on the platform and the buildings on the far right that overlooked the station. The railway arrived in 1852 but this particular station was not opened until 1858. It closed in 1962 and the site was cleared by the end of that decade. Signs from the station were 'saved' by Richard Traves for future display at the Black Country Museum. *(The late Michael Hale)*

Just to the north of Brierley Hill station the railway passed a brickworks that closed at the end of the nineteenth century. This area, between Talbot Street and Bank Street, was reclaimed and new streets were laid out – to be lined with turn-of-the-century houses built by Bishop brothers. The streets included West Street, now Bradleymoor Road, facing the railway, Adelaide Street and Trinity Street. This 2009 view of Adelaide Street is dominated by the presence of the Alexandra Buildings of 1902.

A Halifax bomber, returning from a raid on Germany, crashed into the Adelaide Street area of Brierley Hill in the early hours of 16 March 1944. Mrs Rowbottom, who was staying at her parents' home on that night, was killed and there was extensive damage to property. *(Express & Star)*

Above: Foundation stones were laid for the Temperance Institute in Trinity Street on 11 September 1909. The event raised over £300 towards the £700 cost of construction. It was built by G. Lafford and the architect was Henry Jennings.

It was formally opened on 30 November 1909 by Miss Hooper, the daughter of the local MP, Mr A.G. Hooper, who was also present. Today it has become a nursery. The Temperance Institute was also known as 'the Brotherhood Hall'. The Brotherhood was a temperance society which met at the hall every Saturday evening as a branch of the International Order of Good Templars. For twenty-five years the President of the lodge was David Guttery (see page 28). In 1947 the Temperance Council, who ran the hall, sold it to the Brotherhood for £1,000, but what later happened to the Brotherhood is not clear. The Temperance Council continued to exist until 1965 and then finally gave away its funds. *(NW)*

Right: The Railway Inn was built on the junction of Adelaide Street and Fenton Street and took its name from its proximity to the railway. *(NW)*

The Civic Buildings were a major component in Brierley Hill's plans to modernise and assert its importance. They were constructed in three stages: council offices, civic suite including a council chamber, and finally a public hall capable of seating over 1,000 people. Phase one was completed in 1954. When Brierley Hill joined Dudley in 1966, the council offices became home to the newly created West Midlands Constabulary.

On 25 April 2009 the Dudley MBC St George's Day Parade set off from Brierley Hill Civic Centre on its march through Brierley Hill – making good use of the fact that all road traffic could be diverted to the new ring road. This picture of the parade setting off shows the third and final part of the Civic Centre to be built – the large concert hall – opened by Councillor Mrs Pargeter on 21 September 1957. *(NW)*

Above and below: West Midlands Travel BX09 PCV on the 311 route to Stourbridge sets out from the Dudley Road to cross the top of Level Street and enter Brierley Hill High Street in July 2009. On the left the Liberal Club building carries the date 1902 and the Danilo cinema (seen below when new in 1936) awaits some new use or demolition. At one time this area was the eastern outskirts of Brierley Hill, and the area on the right, east of Level Street, was heavily worked for coal. *(NW)*

Above: Looking towards the screen in the Danilo cinema. On Monday 21 December 1936 George Formby peeped out from between these curtains to announce that it had 'turned out nice again' and to assist Viscount Ednam in opening the cinema. The Danilo lasted until 22 February 1969 when it closed with a screening of *The Graduate*. After closure as a cinema, the Danilo was used as a bingo and social club for many years, and then went through various names and physical modifications in its guise as a nightclub. Even while this book was being prepared, the building, now looking rather forlorn, was put up for auction and sold again. *(H.A. Mason)*

Above and opposite below: Almost opposite the Danilo, at 4 Dudley Road, was Jack Cheadle's record shop – in fact Jack supplied the records played at the Danilo. Jack Cheadle (1905–72) was the son of William Cheadle who had a forge at the back of the Turks Head in the High Street. He was a clever man with electrical matters and ran this shop from just before the Second World War until the mid-1960s. Here is seen here inside his shop and, opposite, by the door. *(John Cheadle)*

Baruch Beckley founded a cycle business in 1888 in this building on the left-hand side of Dudley Road, coming out of town. He became an agent for Sunbeam cycles in 1898 and then started to cater for the motor car. The business passed to his two sons, Ebenezer and Frank, and they continued it until Frank retired in 1962. Note the early type of petrol pump – probably the first in Brierley Hill. *(Graham Beckley Collection)*

Frank and Eb Beckey also opened premises on the other side of Dudley Road, on land that had once been home to a short-lived cinema of 1913 vintage and a dairy. Here we seen their garage decorated for Queen Elizabeth II's Coronation in June 1953. Note the petrol pumps are more modern than the example seen in the picture on the previous page. This building still exists as motor spares warehouse. *(Graham Beckley Collection)*

From John Street a track crossed the railway to the Orchard. The latter was acquired and developed as a sports field by the Round Oak Steel Works Sports & Social Club. Here we see Rachel Powell (see page 48) winning a race on that ground in about 1925. The ground was later used by Brierley Hill Alliance and Dudley Town Football Club but was then redeveloped as a private sports centre. *(Gloria Smith)*

Boys from Brierley Hill Secondary School (Bent Street) put on a fund-raising exhibition at the school in 1967. The main attraction at the show was a large Scalextric model car-racing track, operated here by the organisers, Tim Gresham and Kevin Webb. Ken Hughes took over as head of the Bent Street school in April 1964 but died four years later in June 1968 – one year before the Bent Street boys' school amalgamated with the Brockmoor girls' school to form Brierley Hill County Secondary School, led by Annie Stansfield.

The Bent Street schools were built in 1882 by the Kingswinford School Board, and were enlarged in 1896, for infants (with an entrance in John Street), boys and girls. This picture was taken in 1929, three years before the older girls moved to Brockmoor.

Bent Street boys in about 1920. Joe Smart (See pages 37, 54 and 56) stands second from left in the third row. *(Gloria Smith)*

This time the Bent Street football team of 1924 (winners of the Round Oak Shield) not only features Joe Smart (top left), but next to him is his teacher, David Guttery. David Reginald Guttery (1890–1958) came to the school in 1916 and at this time was secretary to the Brierley Hill & District Schools' Football League. He and his father were associated with the Temperance Hall and the Brotherhood, and took part in a large variety of local civic, educational and cultural activities. *(Gloria Smith)*

The Bent Street Secondary Modern School's first XI or senior team of 1956/57. Left to right: R. Webster, R. Green, M. Ross, W. Timmins, C. Rich, M. Moore, and Mr Thomas. Seated: A. Perry, J. Barker, Mr Wood (headmaster), A. Pinfold, R. Powell. Front row: R. Hill and L. Page, photographed at the school. *(Alan Perry)*

The Bent Street 'intermediate' team, i.e. the first- and second-year pupils of 1954. The teachers are Edgar Hughes and Cyril Wood, and the back row comprises Messrs Underhill, Fairfax, Allen, Martin, Johnson, -?- and Westwood. Middle row: Messrs Bamford, Bell, Perry and Page. Seated: Messrs Webster and Hanbury. *(Alan Perry)*

The Primitive Methodists established themselves at the Round Oak end of town in the 1820s and then built this rather plain chapel in Bent Street. It closed in 1945 and the premises were later used by the St John Ambulance Brigade. It makes an interesting contrast with grandeur of the Wesleyan chapel in Bank Street. *(R. Hood)*

An early 1990s picture of the Sunday School pupils at the Bank Street Chapel shows us George Stevens as superintendent supported by Mavis Dolman, Barbara Maybury and Frances Bloor as Sunday School teachers. *(Ruth Parsonage)*

A Wesleyan Methodist Society was established in Brierley Hill by about 1812 and first met at Samuel Cooper's home in Level Street. The chapel seen here in Bank Street was opened on 11 October 1829 and managed to survive the threat of subsidence and the ravages of time. A substantial restoration was carried out in 1950, and in the mid-1960s other local congregations, Methodist and Congregational, amalgamated with Bank Street with a view to building a new centre. *(Stan Hill Collection)*

The building was demolished in 1969 followed by construction of its modern replacement, which opened on 30 January 1971, designed by Peter Hammond and built by Bruce Tippet. *(NW)*

Left: The interior of the old Bank Street Wesleyan Methodist Chapel was possibly more 'church-like' than 'chapel-like', as can be seen here. *(Ruth Parsonage)*

Below: The 'new' Bank Street building, to be known as Brierley Hill Methodist Church, was opened on 30 January 1971 by the Revd Raymond A. Hawthorne, surrounded here by the rector of Brierley Hill; Fergus Montgomery MP; Alderman and Mrs J.W.R. Rowley (Mayor and Mayoress of Dudley) and Bert Barnett. *(Edith Hawthorne via Kevin Gripton)*

Among the people buried in the churchyard at Bank Street is the Revd John Thomas (1796 –1881) who had been a Christian missionary in the Friendly Islands. On the centenary of his death, 8 February 1981, two members of the Tongan royal family came to Brierley Hill to celebrate the event. The Revd Colin Smith is seen welcoming Captain Tuita and Princess Salote Pilolevu in the churchyard at Bank Street. Geoff Hemming provides the umbrella.

Some of the girls in the Bank Street Methodist Chapel's Guides and Brownies formed a choir, and are seen here on 12 December 1964 when they sang to the retired pensioners from Round Oak Steel Works in the works canteen. *(R.O. Archives)*

In June 2004 ladies from each of the constituent congregations that amalgamated to form the present-day Bank Street line up with a tea-towel designed to commemorate their origins. Left to right are Beryl Totney from Moor Street, Jean Harris from the old Bank Street, Lilian Davis from the Albion Street Congregationalists, Doreen Gripton from Brockmoor, Gladys George from Hill Street and Brenda Hemming from Silver End. Behind them is a window brought along from the old Bank Street chapel. *(NW)*

The 2nd Brierley Hill Girl Guides at Bank Street are seen here presenting a 'Gang Show' in the old Sunday School room, *c.* 1960. Captain Barbara Maybury, who led the troop, is right in the centre of the picture. *(Chris Eaves Collection)*

2

ROUND OAK
INCLUDING THE WALLOWS

Round Oak may only be a small section of Brierley Hill, but it is perhaps the most well known as a result of it being dominated by the Round Oak Steel Works until the early 1980s. Iron works in the area were started by Benjamin Gibbons on the level between the Dudley Canal and Pedmore Road, but in the early 1840s Gibbons relinquished his lease on the property and the trustees of the Earl of Dudley's estate authorised their rebuilding under the guidance of Richard Smith, the trustees' agent. Success with the New Level Ironworks led Richard Smith to plan a new Round Oak Iron Works and construction began in 1855. Production began on 28 August 1857, turning the pig iron produced in the old works into blooms and slabs of finished iron. When demand for iron waned, the works successfully adopted the production of steel.

The area to the west of the main road is known as The Wallows. House building and the extension of Wallows Road now links this area with Pensnett Road. An industrial estate occupies an area which had once been the operational hub of the Earl of Dudley's railway.

The Round Oak Inn, on the corner of John Street, photographed here in 1986, was one of several pubs close to the steelworks. There had been a pub of this name on this site since the 1790s when the road was turnpiked. The 1930s styling and use of black tile was attractive and it is sad to see the building looking derelict in recent times. It was probably designed by Messrs Scott and Clark and opened in 1939. *(NW)*

The Miners Arms, before rebuilt as illustrated on the previous page, is seen here in 1912. This was during a period when the landlord, Alf Tandy, was providing a soup kitchen for striking workers who form a queue stretching down to Round Oak station, visible on the extreme right. Arthur Garbett's shop also appears in the picture. *(Stan Hill Collection)*

Let us imagine we have arrived at Round Oak at the passenger station on the Stourbridge Jct.–Dudley–Wolverhampton line, built as the Oxford, Worcester & Wolverhampton Railway, and opened in 1852. Here we see a Wolverhampton-bound train arriving during the twilight of the passenger service: the summer of 1962. The photograph was taken from the footbridge which linked the platforms and the station buildings built on the Brierley Hill–Dudley main road. *(John Dew)*

Staff at Round Oak station in the 1920s. Joe Smart (see pages 28 and 54) is third from left in the second row. At the time he was a porter, and while doing this job met Rachel Powell (see page 48), his future wife. He later graduated to the rank of signalman and in the bottom picture is seen in Round Oak signal-box. *(Gloria Smith)*

Class 47 locomotive no. 47192 heads for Dudley and Bescot on 18 June 1984, having passed Round Oak signal-box. Although many of the exchange sidings have been removed it is possible to see the route of the Earl of Dudley's railway as it crossed the main line at right angles just north of the signal-box. On the extreme right is the building destined to become the Round Oak Steel Terminal. *(NW)*

The Blue Brick – also opposite the Round Oak Steel Works – seems to have started life as nineteenth-century house. The faience tiling on the front of the building seems to date from 1929. *(NW)*

By the mid-1980s the old offices of the Earl of Dudley's Round Oak Steel Works were only a shell awaiting demolition. They were built in the 1870s alongside the main railway line and facing the Dudley Road, and had been replaced by a modern office building on the other side of the railway which survives today as a hotel. *(NW)*

A drawing of Round Oak Iron Works in 1873 showing the buildings erected in the mid-1850s. The part of the buildings seen on the left survived over a century and became the bloom and billet dressing bay. The Earl of Dudley's railway system is seen passing through the works and making its way to the point where it crossed the O,W&WR's main line on the left, just beyond the signals. *(R.O. Archives)*

The proximity of the steel works to the town is illustrated here in this high-angle view taken in February 1968. The five chimneys above the open-hearth furnaces became a familiar local landmark. *(Express & Star)*

This 1960s aerial view of Round Oak Steel Works helps make sense of it all. Bottom left we can see the Round Oak Inn on the corner of John Street (see page 35). Across the bottom of the picture is Dudley Road heading back towards the town centre past the junctions with John Street and Bent Street. We can see the Dudley Canal snaking its way around the works, and on the extreme right can see where

it passes under Level Street. In the distance is the Queens Head and the lower end of Level Street. It is even possible to discern the slag quarry in the top right of the picture and work out the alignment of the picture on page 56.

Above: By the 1960s many photographs were being taken to record the workers at Round Oak like the one on the right, but here is an example from about 1910. Foreman Attwood, wearing a tie, sits in the centre of the front row. On the left, front row, is John Pearson, a blacksmith and boiler riveter. *(John Pearson)*

Left: John Holland took this atmospheric picture of four furnacemen in 1967 in the open-hearth melting shop. Left to right are Malcolm Crowe (fourth hand melter), Bill Jones (first hand), Charles Tomlinson (second hand) and Brian Hadlington (third hand). Bill Jones had started work at Round Oak in 1918 (the photograph was supplied by his daughter, Ruth Parsonage).

The retirement of Stan Davis of the Works Machine Shop, the last man at Round Oak to complete over fifty years of service. Stan is shaking hands with Terry Lawrence, his supervisor. On the left, in the blazer, is Albert Simcox, Central Engineering Foreman.

George Long, works engineer, shakes hands with 'Alum Bar' Harry – Harry Painter. Many such pictures were taken by Doug Heath, the works photographer (these are from the collection of Colin Storey).

Viv Howells, Chief Engineer, shakes hands with Bob Littlewood at the latter's retirement. Many pictures such as this one were taken by Round Oak's photographer, Douglas Heath, and were reproduced in the staff magazine, *The Acorn*. *(Colin Storey)*

Although Douglas Heath's 'retirement photos' were rather male-dominated as one might expect in a steel works, he did record the work of the female staff at Round Oak, and took photos such as this to show how the works were being modernised and were introducing new technology. In 1967 the company introduced the latest automated data processing and Doug was there to photograph the new machines at work. Punch card technology now seems like something out of the ark, but in 1967 the girls were proud of their skills in operating these machines. They include Lyn Shaw, Gloria Siviter, Jackie Brain, Ann Swift, Susan Ellis and Gill Starkey. *(R.O. Archives)*

In March 1967 Joe Tordoff retired after forty years' service at Round Oak's Erection Department at the Level Street Mill. He is seen here receiving a clock from Mr E. Barker, the Area Engineer. Joe had also worked in the chain-testing department for fifteen years, but his most interesting experience came in 1932, five years after joining Round Oak, when he assisted a film crew in making a film called *Men of Steel*. The British-made feature film also used locations on Teesside but few people have seen the surviving British Film Institute print to tell us how much is seen of Round Oak. *(Ruth Parsonage)*

Round Oak, like the other major Brierley Hill employers, possessed its own football team as part of the sports and social club provision. Other activities included tennis, golf, bowls, theatre-going and a choir. Here we see the 1966/67 football team, which played in the first division of the Birmingham Works AFA. Standing left to right are Bill Mason (manager), John Feerick, John Coleman, Trevor Flavell, Bob Darby, Bill Whitcombe, Mac Greenaway, Arthur Spruce (dressing room attendant) and Charles Cartwright (secretary). Seated are Jim Guy (captain), Ken Feerick, Robert Wheeler (mascot), Ken Smith, Tony Smith and Terry Bradley. *(R.O. Archive)*

Above: A smoky view of the sheds and workshops at The Wallows on 1 June 1951. On the right are the running sheds which dated back to the early days of the Earl of Dudley's railway, and on the left is the Hippodrome (built in 1938 – at the same time as Dudley's new theatre), which replaced the Castle Works as the system's main heavy repair facility.
(A.W. Croughton)

Left: After the fire at the Bromley Grocery Stores in 1938, Gertrude Nicholas (1911–99) worked for thirty years at Weathershields in Birmingham which involved catching an early morning train from Round Oak every day. Here we see her in Wallows Road, where her family (the Whitehouse family) lived. Brierley Hill UDC built a large number of houses in the Dudley Fields/Wallows area during the inter-war period, creating another sub-section of the town in doing so. Top right we glimpse Hartill's shops and the fish and chip shop – once Forrest's, now the Yuyi Dragon.

3

HARTS HILL

Harts Hill was divided into two parts. The larger part was in Dudley and consisted of Vine Street, Chapel Street, Brick Kiln Street, Canal Street and Wood Street, later known as Garrett Street. The smaller part was on the other side of the main road to Dudley and the only turning at the time was Terrace Street. Gordon Crescent was added after the First World War. The Brierley Hill/Dudley boundary ran down the middle of the main road and swung to the east just beyond Canal Street.

This left a number of key 'landmarks' of Harts Hill quite definitely in the Brierley Hill section of the village, namely the tramway depot which later became the bus garage, and the Harts Hill Mission. The latter had been built as a Nonconformist chapel but was sold to the Church of England in 1838 to act as a 'mission' under the wing of St Michael's. It was transferred to St Augustine's, Holly Hall, in 1930 and survived until the 1970s. Harts Hill's other claim to fame is that it was the birthplace of Don and Roy Richardson who later life became the developers of Merry Hill.

As the main road passed through Harts Hill on its way towards Dudley the buildings seemed to have sunk below its level, as seen here in this 1960 photograph of the White Hart and, beyond it, the Mission Church. From 1904 to 1909 the White Hart was run by Zechariah Tordoff who was related to several Tordoffs who lived in the Harts Hill area. (*Fred Bottfield*)

Harts Hill was a heavily industrialised area, as well as a small residential spot on the border of Brierley Hill and Dudley. Messrs Hill & Smith was a major local employer, but their works stood away from everyone else, beyond the canal. The streets of Harts Hill reverberated to the noise of hammers and presses and Dudley Drop Forging Company, seen here in the 1970s. *(Gerald Lowe Collection)*

Rachel Powell was born on 4 April 1915 and grew up in the Brierley Hill part of Harts Hill – in a house next door to Matthew's Timber Yard. She attended Harts Hill school – in the buildings which later became Holly Hal Secondary School – and proved very successful at sport, in particular as a runner, and netball player. She left school at fourteen and went to work at Peacock's in Brierley Hill. After a spell at a Kidderminster carpet factory, she returned to retailing and later worked for many years as an insurance agent. On 6 August 1934 she entered the Miss Dudley competition at the Regent cinema in Dudley and won the title. In this picture she models the swimsuit provided by Selfridges for her appearance in the Miss England contest. Her fame spread, particularly at Marks & Spencer's where she then worked. Rachel married Joe Smart, a local railwayman with impeccable Brierley Hill credentials (see page 56). Their daughter Gloria taught art at Brockmoor Girls School. Rachel died at the age of ninety-four in 2009. *(Gloria Smith)*

Harts Hill United, with Vic Lilley of Garrett Street seated behind a trophy won in the 1930s. The team was started by the United Methodists, ex-New Connexion, who had a tin chapel in Garrett Street, known as the Bethel. The brick Sunday School building of this chapel still survives in industrial use. *(Carol Cobb)*

A few yards from the New Connexion chapel in Garrett Street was the Primitive Methodist chapel in Chapel Street, next to the Cock public house. Here we see a Sunday School anniversary of about 1950. Mr Dabbs was the Sunday School superintendent, and the girls include Margaret Lawson, Pauline Bingham and Anita George whose father repaired TVs, and owned the only set in Brick Kiln Street. *(Marlene Hickman)*

A charity fund-raising bus-cleaning event at Harts Hill bus garage in 1987 – overseen by manager Brian Parry and his deputy Tony McCormack in the back row. Right to left are Maureen Ward, Diane Round, Margaret Neale, Sue Cooper, John Chell, Dr Cushley from Russells Hall Hospital and Marlene Hickman.

The mothers' class from St Augustine's Mission Church, Harts Hill, in about 1950. The ladies include Mrs Hancox, Mrs Williams, Mrs Brown (all in the back row) plus Mrs Eaves, Mrs Wentworth and Mrs Cartwright. The lady on the extreme right was the mission's organist. The organ was hand-pumped by Norman Milner, whose mother kept a general store on the main road in Harts Hill. The mission, like others, was quite independently minded and was overjoyed when able to open its own brand new Sunday School building on 23 June 1934. *(Vera Birch)*

William Cook, on the right, works on Midland Red bus MHA 513 at Harts Hill Garage in the 1950s. William served in both world wars, but had joined Midland Red in 1927 as a driver based at Stourbridge. After the Second World War he rejoined Midland Red as an engineer at Harts Hill where he stayed until retirement in 1963. *(Robert Cook)*

This picture of a mass meeting outside Harts Hill bus garage provides us with a glimpse of the travel shop and offices built in front of the garage. *(Robert Cook)*

Harts Hill children photographed at a 1953 Coronation party in the Tap Room at the Three Horseshoes pub in Brick Kiln Street. Marlene and Vic Cooper, the children of the licensee are in the centre of the front row. The pub closed about five years after this picture was taken. *(Marlene Hickman)*

The 1958 football team at the Harts Hill Secondary School with teachers Mr Greenaway (left), Mr Cook (middle) and Mr Parkins (right). The school was in the Dudley part of Harts Hill and later changed its name to Holly Hall Secondary School. The latter was replaced by a new school at Scotts Green in the 1960s. *(Vic Cooper)*

4

LEVEL STREET
& MERRY HILL

Merry Hill itself was a high piece of ground near Quarry Bank overlooking the site of the modern shopping complex that has taken its name. The complex occupies the basin of the Tipsyford Brook, a tributary of the Black Brook – an area laid waste by mining in the first half of the nineteenth century. By the second half of the twentieth century some of the 'waste' was farmed, creating a contrasting landscape to the nearby industrial landscape of the Round Oak Steel Works. Access to this area from Brierley Hill was via Level Street which wandered downhill from the town's High Street, at the Civic Centre end, to Pedmore Road. The Levels, from which the street took its name, were terraces used to accommodate the expansion of the steel works; the term was not used to indicate that the road itself was 'level' – which it certainly was not.

The top end of Level Street was another of those micro-communities encountered so often in the Black Country, although very little remains to remind us of its former existence. We include a couple of pictures to acknowledge the present-day presence of the Merry Hill shopping complex in the area around and beyond The Levels.

This rather poorly copied picture is all we have to show the houses in Level Street that once stood opposite the Bush public house. There were also many small houses with a Level Street address that were tucked away in 'folds' behind Level Street – between the end of Pearson Street and derelict open land traversed by the Earl of Dudley's railway and the Dudley Canal. (*Maureen Dean*)

Left: It is difficult to imagine that substantial late Victorian or early Edwardian houses were once to be found at the top of Level Street. Joe Smart, who graduated from working in the quarry at the foot of Level Street to becoming a smallholder and then property owner, moved into one of these houses and here we see his wife, Sarah Ann, standing by the gate of no. 45 Level Street. Joe Smart Junior who features in several pictures used in this book was the last of five children, born when Sarah was thirty-eight. *(Gloria Smith)*

Below: The families living in the Level Street area were largely intermarried, and many of the menfolk worked at Round Oak Steel Works, but the community was dispersed as a result of post-war slum clearance and many moved to new council housing in Brockmoor. Here we see Aynuk Onions marrying Betty Williams in about 1948 surrounded by Level Street children. *(Maureen Dean)*

During the descent of Level Street one came to the Three Furnaces, a Hanson's pub of about 1850 vintage, photographed here in the 1970s. On the other side of Level Street was the Bush that survived until recently as a pine furniture business. Note the floodlight mast in the background – used to light the sidings on the steelworks' railway system. *(Stan Hill Collection)*

Just below the Three Furnaces, Level Street was crossed by the Earl of Dudley's railway and then the Dudley Canal. Today one also passes the Copthorne Hotel at this point and the Merry Hill shopping centre comes into view. On 2 May 1959 the photographer recorded one of the Earl of Dudley's Barclay 0–4–0STs hauling an empty cauldron wagon back across the road after tipping molten slag in the area to the right. Straight ahead, behind the smoke, we look across to the hill on which stands Netherton Church. *(Peter Shoesmith)*

The lower end of Level Street was dominated by the Queens Head below which was another scattered settlement between the industrial waste and the pits. Just before reaching Pedmore Road, Level Street crossed the boundary from Brierley Hill into Dudley, but beyond the Tipsyford Bridge, where the Earl of Dudley's railway passed under Pedmore Road, the Brierley Hill boundary occupied the centre of Pedmore Road – putting the Robin Hood pub firmly in Brierley Hill! This picture looks from the Pedmore Road back up The Levels towards Round Oak Steel Works. Behind the scrapyard in the foreground we can se a mountain of slag that has been quarried to create a gap through which we can see the Queens Head – which survives today as the Millennium nightclub. Take a look at the picture at the foot of the opposite page to gain a sense of just how much this area has changed with the arrival of the Merry Hill complex. *(Express & Star)*

In the 1900s Joe Smart (front left) became foreman in a quarry reclaiming furnace waste for roadstone near the lower end of Level Street. He bought a smallholding near Pedmore Road. We follow the fortunes of his son Joe (Jnr) on page 37, and his daughter Lydia on page 98. One of Joe Jnr's childhood pastimes was playing with the monkeys kept at the Queens Head! *(Gloria Smith)*

The Robin Hood stood on the Pedmore Road, close to Saltwells Wood and the point where the boundaries of Brierley Hill, Dudley and Quarry Bank met. In the nineteenth century it was a refuge for town-dwellers looking for a destination for their walk into the countryside, despite being so close to the industrialised and residential areas. Here we see classic cars in the Robin Hood's car park in the autumn of 1998. *(NW)*

These controversial signs, proclaiming that the Merry Hill shopping complex was the 'town centre' of Brierley Hill, appeared in 2002. The buildings of the Waterfront have dominated the skyline since the mid-1990s and Level Street has become a vast highway. McDonald's, on the right, occupies the approximate site of the slag quarry seen on the opposite page. *(NW)*

The Richardson Brothers took possession of the Round Oak works and the ground behind it in 1983 and the development of the Merry Hill shopping centre began. This mall was two years old when photographed in 1987 but still seemed very 'new'. The malls were sold to Chelsfield in 1998, and on to Westfield in 2004. *(NW)*

Mount Pleasant Primary School choir took part in the School Choir Competition at Merry Hill on 11 December 2009, which they subsequently won. Spectators seen on the balcony above the choir make it clear that this intersection of the malls provides a 'natural' amphitheatre for both commercial and community use in the centre. *(NW)*

5

QUARRY BANK

Of all the constituents of Brierley Hill, Quarry Bank seems to be the most separate and independent. This is reflected in the fact that from 1894 until 1934 it enjoyed running its own affairs under the flag of Quarry Bank Urban District Council.

The 'bank' of Quarry Bank is a ridge that runs from the parish church to the Birch Tree pub at the end of Amblecote Road. Quarry Bank grew up around the crossroads, close to the Blue Ball, where this ridge was crossed by the Dudley–Worcester turnpike road. From various positions quite close to this crossroads, including the Merry Hill which gave the nearby shopping complex its name, it is possible to feel quite close to Brierley Hill because the skyline now dominated by the Waterfront buildings was once dominated by the outline of Round Oak Steel Works. Road connection with the centre of Brierley Hill was via Mill Street, quite a way from the Blue Ball crossroads.

In reality Quarry Bank was always separated from Brierley Hill by open wedges of green space: the bank descended by The Delph Locks on one side of Mill Street and the basin of the Tipsyford Brook which occupied the space between Mill Street and Pedmore Road.

Quarry Bank may seem like one of those places that has enjoyed an independent existence but decimalisation came to the town on Monday 15 January 1971 just like everywhere else! Here we see Mr Perry of Quarry Bank Junior School preparing locals for the great day. *(Gwen Perry via Geoff Tristram)*

A NEW APPROACH TO QUARRY BANK

In previous books about Quarry Bank we have defined the township by using the boundaries of the Quarry Bank Urban District – which began life in 1894 and lasted until 1934 when absorbed by Brierley Hill. During that period the town was physically separated from its neighbours in a way that recent greater urbanisation has destroyed. Quarry Bank consisted of the four communities that occupied the quadrants of a circle that centred around the crossroads by the Blue Ball.

However, in this book we are looking at Quarry Bank from a Brierley Hill-centred viewpoint. Brierley Hill stretched southwards along Mill Street but at the junction with Two Woods Lane it struck the boundary of Quarry Bank. From then on the boundary ran along the centre of the road – putting the Cottage Spring (see page 86) in Brierley Hill, but the houses opposite in Quarry Bank.

The area between Two Woods Lane and Mount Pleasant forms yet another sub-section of Quarry Bank with a history of its own. A glance at the 1903 map shows the area between Two Woods Lane and the Old Level Iron Works as an empty wilderness – a desert created by mining for coal at Pits nos 28 and 35 of the Earl of Dudley's Saltwells Colliery – rapidly returning to nature but virtually uninhabited. South of Two Woods Lane, and safely inside Quarry Bank Urban District, the land was divided into many small units and there were scattered houses among the disused mine shafts and small works. Talbot's Lane, at right angles to Mount Pleasant, was an interesting survivor of that world and only disappeared at the end of the 1960s when the surrounding industrial estate engulfed it and created a new Talbot's Lane.

In 1828 land was bought by one Thomas Stanley, and his daughter Mary married a Benjamin Talbott, introducing the name – then spelt with two 'Ts' – to the area. One of their daughters married a Weaver, and had a son, George Talbot Weaver, who lived in Talbot Lane until its was sold in about 1969 for redevelopment. His children, who are alive today, can provide an insight into life in Talbot Lane in its last days.

Mike and Phil James look across Thomas' Farm from Two Woods Lane towards Round Oak Steel Works in about 1980 – before the Merry Hill shopping complex was built. Colliery waste in the foreground has become green enough to be called a farm – contrasting with the bare banks in the middle distance where furnace slag was being tipped. *(John James)*

Above: A view from Talbot's Lane of nos 2 and 3, possibly taken in the 1870s. The ladies are Mrs Jane Weaver and Miss Lizzie Talbot. No. 2 is closest to the camera, and beyond is no. 3 which was built for Jane and her husband. No. 2 became dilapidated but no. 3 survived as the family home until 1969.

Right: In this picture we are looking along the line of the Talbot Lane cottages in the opposite direction in 1968. Left to right are John, Jane holding her niece Sarah, and Mary Weaver. *(Mary Jones)*

Construction of Christ Church Quarry Bank began in October 1845 and the building was consecrated on 2 March 1847. This was part of a decade of breaking up the ancient parish of Kingswinford in recognition that places like Brierley Hill, Brockmoor, Pensnett and Quarry Bank had grown sufficiently to need their own parish churches. It was also recognition that the Nonconformists were already well established in such areas. Christ Church occupies a good central position in Quarry Bank, close to the key crossroads around which the town has developed, and close to the High Street, and has played an important part in the lives of local people and events in the town's history. Today it no longer has a church hall or a Sunday School and the vicar is part of a 'team ministry'. *(NW)*

The Church Hall in Quarry Bank had a history completely wrapped up in the story of the district. It began life as a small nail warehouse at the end of the eighteenth century, and was close to the Sheffield Street area where many nailers lived and worked. In the early 1840s it was sold to the trustees of the Primitive Methodist congregation, but they decided to build a chapel in New Street. In 1844 it was acquired by the Church of England and was used for services until Christ Church was completed in 1847. It then became the Sunday School, and was also used as a church day school. In 1913 it was substantially rebuilt as a church hall and is seen here in late 1959 when the site in the foreground was being prepared to house a new community centre. It was demolished in the late 1990s. *(Philip Millward)*

Vicar George Larkin with a post-war Christ Church Sunday School outing. He was vicar of Quarry Bank from 1946 until 1972. Sunday School parades, outings and anniversaries were once major events in all the townships of Brierley Hill. *(MPLHG)*

When the Kingswinford School Board began surveying the educational facilities and needs of the Quarry Bank area, they found a church school operating in the building seen opposite but hoped that they could replace that by building a new Board School in the High Street. This was opened in 1872 and was extended in 1877 and 1881. The 1877/81 building was replaced in 1937 by the building seen here – with provision for boys on the ground floor and girls upstairs although it now operates as a mixed junior school. It was a typical 1930s linear structure with open-sided corridors and the two halls provided in a right-angled extension. This is now regarded as life-expired and a new school is planned on this site. *(NW)*

Mr Ivan Badger was headmaster of the boys' elementary school in Quarry Bank for many years and then transferred to the new secondary school in 1932. He retired in 1938. He was a keen sportsman and is seen here with his school's cricket team.

The senior lads at Coppice Lane Secondary School for Boys pose for a picture with their teacher John Watt in about 1961/62. The secondary schools in Coppice Lane – for boys on one side of the road, and for girls on the other – opened in October 1932. Ivan Badger transferred from the boys' elementary school to run the boys' secondary school and Florence Wooldridge came to lead the girls. The schools merged in 1969 and evolved into the Thorns School in the 1970s. *(Dennis Rydes)*

Quarry Bank Junior School football team of the 1962/63 season, accompanied by Ray Weston (deputy head), Iain Lewis and Mr Perry, the headmaster. Robert Glaze, bottom right, later played for Aston Villa. *(Gwen Perry via Geoff Tristram)*

The same staff at Quarry Bank Junior School pose for a photograph with the athletics team of the early 1960s. The team includes David Potter, Stephen Plant, David Booth, David Raybould, Geoffrey Weaver and David Homer, whose father ran the Homer's Coach Company. Behind the trees is the smallholding reached from Rose Hill. *(Gwen Perry via Geoff Tristram)*

Mount Pleasant Primary School was the second to be established by the Board in Quarry Bank. It began life in the Wesleyan Chapel Sunday School in 1882 and moved to this site in 1888. The gable just before the spire carries a Kingswinford School Board plaque of 1888 vintage. Coming towards the camera we see the new buildings added in 1992, and on the extreme right the new hall which replaced an old clinic and home of 'Killer' Kelly, the school's dentist. *(NW)*

Mr W. Hunt, a resident of Brockmoor, was Mount Pleasant's first headmaster and he stayed from 1888 until 1930. Here we see him with the 1920 football team. He died in 1939 and is buried in Brockmoor churchyard close to where he was born. *(MPLHG)*

Mount Pleasant school was proud of its recorder ensemble led and organised by Mrs Hilda Mantle. She joined the staff at Mount Pleasant in 1945 and during the 1950s her recorder group gave many local concerts – seen here at Kinver church. She also 'twinned' her class with a school in America. Mrs Mantle died in 2002, aged over 100. *(June Ashmore)*

To the left of this picture one can see Thorns Primary School, opened in 1969, and in the centre of the picture is Thorns Community College. Secondary education had been provided in Quarry Bank by separate boys' and girls' schools in Coppice Lane. They amalgamated in 1969 and developed into Thorns Comprehensive School and made a staged removal to this site in Stockwell Road. *(David Hughes/Phillip Millward)*

Quarry Bank's population began to grow in the nineteenth century as chainmakers and colliers settled in the area but the town later became associated with the holloware trade. Pressing, fabricating, welding, galvanising and enamelling became the skills of the local workforce, making everything from bins and buckets to teapots and bread bins. In May 2009 Lynda Waltho MP called in to see Bird Stevens and its 54-strong multi-skilled workforce still exploiting modern versions of those skills. Here she is greeted by John Wallett, press shop manager, and the MD, Steve Ruston. The firm was founded at the Sun Works, between Sun Street and Merry Hill in 1913. (*Express & Star*)

Several Quarry Bank firms produced galvanised hollowware, including John Stringer's Tubular Holloware of Oak Street, and John Stevens' Jury Holloware of Thorn's Road. Here we see Messrs Brettell & Shaw proudly displaying their products at a 1950s industry fair. The Rhodesia Works, where these were made, was in West Street and was built by the famous local builders Arthur Webb & Sons. Today houses built by another local builder, Cox's, occupy the site.
(*John Shaw*)

Quarry Bank has been a sufficiently independent community to build its own cultural institutions and sports clubs quite separate from those of Brierley Hill. The Quarry Bank Operatic Society is seen here celebrating its 50th anniversary in 2010, but it can trace its history back beyond that fifty years. When QBOS was formed by Edgar and Bessie Cartwright, Tom and Sybil Genner, Vera Dunn, Joyce Capewell, Doreen Nicklin and Brian Clark in 1960, they were carrying on a tradition established by the Cradley Forge Amateur Operatic & Dramatic Society that had been started to help raise funds to build the Cradley Forge chapel of 1928. Here we see Doreen Nicklin, now society chairperson, cutting the anniversary cake with Tommy Mundon, the society's president, in Quarry Bank's Community Centre. *(Express & Star)*

During 2009 Quarry Bank lost its post office, its local 'estate office', and its library, proudly opened by Brierley Hill UDC seventy years earlier. The local Community Centre, opened by BHUDC on 10 May 1961, survives – for the time being – and is seen here on 12 January 2009 when a minimal 'library link' service was being opened in the building to replace the 'proper' library. Brian Genner points out that the opening is late! *(NW)*

The Nonconformists have been well represented in Quarry Bank. The Wesleyan Methodists opened their chapel in Mount Pleasant as early as 1828. The Primitive Methodists built chapels in Birch Coppice and New Street. The New Connexion Methodists used chapels at Cradley Forge and Mount Pleasant, and a Pentecostal 'temple' was to be found near Two Woods Lane. An independent fellowship met at the Soap Works until building this chapel in Z Street in 1897. They became Congregationalists and in 1935 built a new church in the High Street. *(Alan Southall)*

In 1967 the Congregationalists opened a new Sunday School building adjacent to their church in the High Street. This made the 1897 building in Z Street – seen behind the new Sunday School – redundant, and the site is now occupied by a car park. In the 1960s many Congregational churches joined with the Presbyterians in forming the United Reformed Church but not in Quarry Bank! *(Alan Southall)*

Many Nonconformist chapels did not have a license to perform marriages, but gradually the Anglican monopoly was broken and in the book *Quarry Bank & The Delph in Old Photographs* we featured two first weddings at Quarry Bank chapels. Here is a third! Alan Southall married Jill Hall on 29 January 1966 – the first wedding at the Congregational chapel in the High Street. Left to right are Gillian Bishop, Vivian Priest, Nellie Southall, David Penn, the groom and bride, Laura Hall, Sam Bradley, Joan Bradley and Lorraine Downton. *(Alan Southall)*

Quarry Bank Junior School using the Congregational church to present their Nativity play. *(Gwen Perry)*

Quarry Bank's most famous football team was Quarry Bank Celtic, the history of which is outlined in *What's Happened to Quarry Bank?*, but Quarry Bank has also been home to many school teams and pub teams. Here is Three Horseshoes Athletic in about 1981, based at the pub at the lower end of the High Street (private housing is now on the site). In the back row are Messrs Parsons, Passmore, Dunn, Attwood, Raybould, Bradley, Harris, Cullis, Wood, Genner, Wilcox and Bradley. In the front row are Messrs Haynes, Attwood, Raybould, Handley, Robinson, Pell, Homer, Pell, Moore, Dunn and Wood. Neil Moore, by the ball, went on to play for Halesowen Town and even appeared at Wembley! When the pub closed the team moved to the Cottage in the Bower, until that also closed. *(Martin Pell Collection)*

Quarry Bank produced its own 'stars' of the local entertainment scene. Ernie Webb (1907–92) was typical of such talent. He had a strong stage presence, particularly in comic roles, but could also sing and dance. He appeared in, wrote and directed many of the shows presented by the Cradley Forge Amateur Operatic & Dramatic Society – the forerunner of the Quarry Bank Society featured on page 69. Ernie continued to live in Quarry Bank, but later used his talents with the amateur operatic society based in Cradley Heath – when this picture was taken. *(Author's Collection)*

6

MILL STREET
TO QUARRY BANK

Mill Street starts out from Five Ways as very much a 'town centre' street with an interesting cluster of small shops and pubs, but once it crosses the new bypass it becomes a main artery between Brierley Hill and Quarry Bank. It contains two contrasting schools – one with an interesting selection of buildings dating from 1910, and every decade since, and another in the modern idiom.

Mill Street crosses the Dudley Canal at the top of The Delph Locks, and a fine view of them is obtained from the bridge. Many people will also know this spot as an access and exit to and from the Merry Hill shopping complex. For the history-conscious explorer, Mill Street provides access to the Nine Locks Colliery, made famous by an accident, and to the site of a sawmill of which there is now no trace. Close to the sawmills, there were once brickworks on both sides of the road – the Nine Locks Brickworks and the Endurance Brickworks. The marl holes and pitbanks once provided open space between Brierley Hill and Quarry Bank, but ribbon development along Mill Street, and developments like the Corbett Road estate have obscured all this.

The Alma, a typical 1930s pub, stood on the corner of Mill Street, but by the time this picture was taken in the 1970s, it had become 'The Teaser' – a name given to one of the members of a team of glassmakers. It has since been a Chinese restaurant and a steak house. *(John James)*

Left: Next door to the Alma in Mill Street was a small bakery shop, started by the Myatts after the First World War. It was passed on to the Waltons and the Rounds, and to the Potters – as seen here – before finally closing as bakery in 2008. The Potters produced their bread and cakes from their bakehouse on Commonside, Pensnett. Black Country Micros occupies the first of a terrace of small shops that in the 1930s had been known as the Bright Home Stores, owned by the Lowther family. *(Jimmy Potter)*

Below: Two small pubs, built in the traditional Black Country two-bay style still exist in the first stretch of Mill Street: The Kings Head and The Waterloo. The latter's name gives an indication of its antiquity, and in the 1970s it featured in a *Good Beer Guide*. It now finds itself standing on the corner of the new bypass, opened on 6 November 2008.

Above: Near the junction of Mill Street and Cottage Street was the tall brick engine-house building of the Locks Lane Colliery, photographed in about 1977 shortly before its demolition. In March 1869 this was the site of the Nine Locks pit disaster, when thirteen colliers were trapped in the mine for several days. Twelve were rescued and thus survived the disaster. After the pit closed, water was still pumped up to the surface and was piped to Marsh & Baxter's factory as a coolant. *(Keith Hodgkins)*

THUNDER STORM IN BRIERLEY·HILL,

APRIL 25TH, 1894.

Showing Damage done to Stack.

Locks' Lane Stack.

Reprinted from the "Brierley-Hill and Stourbridge Advertiser," April 28th.

Photographed by D. Dixon, Brierley-Hill.

Right: As can be seen from this postcard, the chimney stack adjacent to the Locks Lane engine-house also acquired fame in April 1894 after being struck by lightning. *(Stan Hill Collection)*

As Mill Street descends to the bridge over the canal at the top of the Nine Locks it passes the Mill Street schools. The first school to open on this site was the Mill Street County Girls School which opened on 22 August 1910, with Miss Parnell in charge. She and the pupils had moved in from the former National school in Hill Street, and occupied buildings at the rear of the present site. This building, bearing the date 1928, was erected in anticipation of accommodating older pupils. *(NW)*

By the 1930s there were many pupils interested in staying on at school beyond the minimum leaving age of fourteen, and provision was made for them on the Mill Street site by opening the Brierley Hill Intermediate School in August 1931. Staff and pupils are photographed here in a classic school panorama of May 1936. The Intermediate School which had functioned since 1931 was later known as the Commercial School, although from 1947 onwards it was designated as a secondary technical school. Because entry was by selection (the 11-plus) the school was eventually given grammar school status. *(School Archive)*

In 1985 the Junior School then on the site held a 75th anniversary celebration, organised by headmaster Alan Rowe. Mill Street first became a mixed junior school on 23 June 1930. Here we see four of the 1985 pupils dressed in the fashions of earlier decades: Ian Skelding and Lisa Gregg representing the 1920–45 period, and Julie Yates and Angela Thursfield representing an earlier period. Many ex-pupils were contacted, the earliest of which could recall the opening of the school. *(School Archive)*

Members of the 1985 staff, with headmaster Alan Rowe who had worked hard to record the school's history to celebrate its 75th anniversary. *(School Archives)*

Above and below: In 1930 the Mill Street school became a junior mixed school and became well known for its musical achievements. In May 1934 these children won a First Class Certificate in the Stafford County Musical Association's annual festival. Such large-scale productions were popular, and below, we can see the cast of a later production of the *Pied Piper of Hamelin*. The infants at Hill Street school did not make a transfer to the Mill Street site until 1937. By that time older children on the site who did not graduate to the Intermediate School were transferring to Brockmoor (girls) and Bent Street (boys).

Once the Brierley Hill Grammar School pupils had moved out of Mill Street to their new purpose-built home at Crestwood, the Mill Street premises could be developed as solely a junior school with adjoining infants and nursery departments. Here we see changes being made to the playground in 1983 to provide facilities for the nursery children. Adrian Menner and David Pearson put the finishing touches to a playground snake.

Back in 1974 Patricia Barrington and Michelle Picken present encyclopedias to the school having won them at the Royal Show at Stoneleigh the previous year.

Above and below: Mill Street Junior School football team of 1951/52, and the swimming team of 1967 with Mr D'Arcy Jones. The swimming team always did well in Brierley Hill school competitions because the school's proximity to the new baths, opened in 1961, enabled them to have extra practice at lunchtime! *(School Archive)*

Mr Lester's class at the Mill Street school in 1958/9 when it was still known as the Commercial School. Back row, left to right, are John Pain, John Worton, Alan Thompson, Trevor Randle, Ivan Williams, Chris George, Alan Hill, Malcolm Miles and Robert Russell. Middle row: Reg Handy, Michael Roper, Paul ?, Pat Wood, Rosalind Share, Barbara Lloyd, Elizabeth Leatherbarrow, David Oakley, David Harvey, Mike Roberts. Front row: Glenys Marsh, Joan Stinton, Ann Shemwell, Ann Timmins, Mr Lester, Jean Little, Sheila Stanton, Cynthia Miles, Rosalind Moore and Diane Spall. *(School Archives)*

Mrs Butler's form 2 of 1955 at the Mill Street Commercial School. The Day School for Commerce was the foundation from which the Brierley Hill Grammar School developed. The latter finally materialised with the completion of new facilities in Bromley Lane. *(School Archives)*

The staff at Mill Street school in about 1956, featuring the headmaster, Mr D'Arcy Jones who had left Mount Pleasant school, Quarry Bank, in 1954 to come to Mill Street. D'Arcy Jones was well known for his interest in amateur dramatics. Also on view is Viv Yates (top left, deputy head) and Ray Weston (top right, founder of Cum Sing wi' We). *(Stan Hill Collection)*

A class at Mill Street Primary School in about 1954. Many of these children can be identified but space makes it impossible to name them all. They came from The Delph and the streets that disappeared under the Chapel Street redevelopment. On the front row, Tony Whittaker sits on the left, and third from right is John Murray whose parents kept the Rocks Tavern at the top of Rocks Hill. The path at the back led from the Promenade to the school gate. *(Joan Brookes Collection – who, as Joan Gillam, is third from left on back row)*

Form 1/2 in 1958 – the last intake of Brierley Hill Grammar School pupils to start their secondary education on the Mill Street site as, in 1959, the school moved to the new building at Crestwood. Only the girls have been identified: second row: Jayne Juliard, Margaret Hopkins, Sheila ?, Patricia Raybould, Christine Perry and Janet Keeler. Front row: Gillian Plant, Carol Jones, Jennifer Nash, Maureen Johnson, Barbara Knott, Ann Millinship, Mr R. O'Brian, Lynne Raybould, Susan Mobberley, Christine Jones, Norma ? and Janette Hinton. *(Chris Eaves Collection)*

Just below the Mill Street schools the road crosses the Dudley Canal and the view to the south-west from this bridge once looked like this. A horse-drawn boat is seen climbing The Delph Locks in the mid-1950s, when the skyline still included the chimneys of brickworks in The Delph. Today thick trees obscure the original line of the canal to the left, the stables, and the pounds to the right. *(Bill Bawden)*

From the opposite parapet of the Mill Street bridge the canal threaded its way between an iron works (on the left) and a bucket and galvanising works on the right, beyond which was a wharf for boats belonging to the London, Midland & Scottish Railway. Close to the wharf was a cottage in which the Handy Angle Manufacturing Co. was founded in 1951 by J.E. Kinnear and his son Peter. Reinvented as Link 51, they moved into this new warehouse in 1986. The facility was opened by Kenneth Baker. It now flanks the road providing access from Mill Street to the Merry Hill complex.

The Handy Angle ladies' football team were pioneers of ladies' football and are seen here in 1957. Top left is Harry Rydes, the team's trainer, and in the middle of the front row is their captain, Joan Grocott. Players include Margaret Parkes and Margeret Bradley. *(Carol Cobb)*

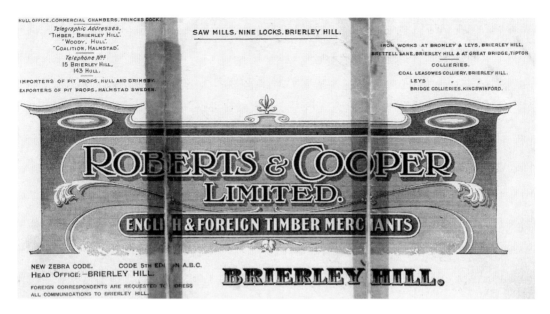

At one time, just on the Quarry Bank side of the Delph Locks, Messrs Roberts & Cooper had a sawmill which was headquarters of their timber business – as seen from this heading to a piece of notepaper used in 1913. The heading also informs us that they had ironworks at Bromley and The Leys, and three local collieries, and probably made bricks. *(Graham Beckley Collection)*

St Mary's Roman Catholic Primary School opened on the Mill Street site in the autumn of 1964. It replaced the original premises built behind St Mary's Church, and the school's opening was marked by marching from the old premises to the new ones. The school was extended in 1973. Ms A. Maher (headteacher) is seen here in front of the school in 2010. *(John James)*

The Cottage Spring was a Hanson's pub but in recent times has been run by an independent brewer. It was designed by local architect Henry Jennings in the 1900s and compares well with his other surviving designs such as the Temperance Hall and Walter Smith's High Street shop. *(Stan Hill Collection)*

Two Woods Lane is a turning to the right from Mill Street just before it reaches the Amblecote Road. The lane ran across to Pedmore Road, forming the boundary of Quarry Bank. At the far end of Two Woods Lane it was possible to gaze across these fields, once colliery waste, towards the Chapel Street flats. The Merry Hill shopping complex now fills this space and a dense high hedge runs along the line of the fence in the foreground. This photograph was taken in about 1980. *(John James)*

7

DOWN TO
THE DELPH

J ust as the northern end of Brierley Hill descended via The Levels into the basin of the Tipsyford
Brook, the southern end of Brierley Hill descended steeply into an area originally drained by the
Colbourne Brook. The ground rose again on the far side of these basins forming a ridge that ran
from Quarry Bank to the Amblecote Road.

In this chapter we look at the area that descended into The Delph – an area now dominated by the
Chapel Street flats, but once occupied by roads like South Street, New Street, Hill Street, Dean Street,
Potter Street and Chapel Street itself. At the foot of the slope Delph Road made its way from the Mount
Pleasant end of Quarry Bank across to Silver End.

The Delph developed as a community in its own right – previously explored in *Quarry Bank & The
Delph* (The History Press, 2009). We look at it again here briefly before continuing our journey to Silver
End.

Looking down New Street in May 1956 we see the way in which Brierley Hill fell away
dramatically into The Delph. The town's gasworks dominate the area at the foot of the hill and
beyond it are the brickyards and fireclay mines collieries of the area. The three lads running
uphill are David and Robert Rounds, and their friend, Trevor Nicholls. *(Express & Star)*

Brierley Hill was directly linked to The Delph via Hill Street, seen here in the 1950s, and the steps that led down Rock Hill. Today Hill Street is a wide open thoroughfare that joins the bypass at end of the High Street and provides access to the Chapel Lane flats. Here we are on the corner of Dean Street, looking towards Potter Street and the top of Rocks Hill, with just an intriguing glimpse of the Hill Street Methodist Chapel on the right. The chapel closed in 1965 when the congregation joined their colleagues in Bank Street. *(MPLHG)*

A 1950s view of the bottom of Hill Street seen from Potters Lane. The Rock Hill Steps would be on the right. The dilapidation of the buildings suggests the reason for clearing this area and embarking on the huge Chapel Street scheme. *(Gloria Smith)*

Above: Looking up the hill towards the Promenade, and on the left Chapel Street, April 1963. At this time, demolition was proceeding while new homes were being built. In the area used by the contractor's huts, steps had continued down the hill from Chapel Street to one or two properties on the hillside. *(Express & Star/John Pearson)*

Right: The Chapel Street scheme was very ambitious and led to dramatic and widescale demolition of the streets that straddled the steep drop from Brierley Hill into The Delph. Here we see Mary Coley's little shop in Hill Street in the 1950s – a decade before the sweeping changes took effect. Mary, who was the sister of Joe Smart (page 37), is joined by her husband Arthur, a life-long local railwayman. *(Gloria Smith)*

Early in the twentieth century the Promenade was created, running between Mill Street and Chapel Street. Here we look down on it from the top of Brick Kiln Court, the easternmost of the Chapel Street flats. Instead of looking out over small pits and brickyards beyond Delph Road we now look out over the Withymoor Village. *(NW)*

This Edwardian postcard provides us with a view from The Delph looking up the locks towards Mill Street. Nine locks originally brought the Dudley Canal down to The Delph where an 'end-on' junction was made with the Stourbridge Canal in 1779. The flight was re-aligned, using only eight locks, in the 1850s. *(Michael Reuter)*

Above: Looking across The Delph towards Amblecote Road in the 1900s. In the foreground are the small pits in which both coal and fireclay could be mined. Small tramroads provided transport to the nearby brickworks. *(Michael Reuter)*

Right: The Delph was home to workers in the brickyards and associated pits that filled a vast area between Delph Road and Amblecote. A variety of workers gather here to inspect the damage to the Mill House at The Delph Brickworks (E.J. & J. Pearson's) after the fire of 13 August 1913. *(MPLHG)*

Almost as famous as The Delph Locks was the little wooden mission church built in 1886 in the middle of The Delph. It became a symbol of the area's independent spirit and money was collected with a view to replacing it with a more permanent building. Closure came in 1952 and it was not replaced. *(Express & Star)*

CERTIFICATE OF BAPTISM.

Solemnized in the 'WESLEYAN REFORM UNION CHURCH, *Delph*

In the County of *Staffordshire* in the year 19*21*

| When Baptized. | Child's Name; Son or Daughter. | Parents' Name. | | Abode. | Child's Age when Baptized. | The Minister by whom the Baptism was solemnized. |
		Christian.	Surname.			
19*21* *March 27* *No.15*	*Son*	*William Henry Alice*	*Timmins* *Timmins*	*25 South Street Bradley Hill*	*8 day of March 5 Weeks Old*	*B. Hewins*

I Certify that the above is a true copy of an entry in the Register-Book for Baptisms, solemnized in the

Wesleyan Reform Union Church *Delph* in the County of *Staffordshire*

B. Hewins

Wesleyan Reform Union Minister.

A Wesleyan Reform chapel also once existed in The Delph although it seems to have disappeared without trace just beyond the reach of living memory. It can be seen on the 1900 map of The Delph and was sited just by the canal bridge – opposite the Bell. This surviving baptism certificate proves it was still 'in business' in 1921, when the minister was the Revd B. Hewins. The present-day Wesleyan Reform Union has no record of the chapel's existence. *(Carol Cobb)*

An early 1960s view of Lower Delph Road as seen from the junction with Potter Street/New Street, looking towards Delph Bridge and the Bell public house. Behind the late Victorian houses on the right was an older terrace, and a pub, long since vanished, close to the canal. *(Michael Reuter)*

Turning to look in the other direction, we look along Delph Road towards the bend in the road at the junction with South Street. You can just make out the trees in the hillside churchyard of South Street Baptist church. The little corner shop on the left was run by Hilda Dunn. These buildings were built later than those seen above, and prevent us seeing the gas works behind them. *(Michael Reuter)*

The Delph had its one football team in the shape of The Delph Rovers, based at the Black Horse in the early 1960s. They played in the Kidderminster League Division Four. They trained on a park at Silver End, and played home matches on Wordsley Park. In the back row are J. Allcock (secretary), M. Roberts, J. Turley, W. Bentley, E. Trotter, P. Cunneen, D. Baker and E. Brazier (manager). Front row: -?-, -?-, R. Bridge, R. Hale, P. Davies, M. Davies, -?-. *(Peter Davies)*

The Black Horse as it was in the 1960s. Since then the pubs of The Delph have become better known. The tour could start at the Bell and take in the Ninth Lock (once the Stores), the Duck & Iron, the Black Horse, and the Vine – better known as the Tenth Lock. *(Stan Hill Collection)*

8

SILVER END, BRETTELL LANE & HAWBUSH

If we continue westwards along Lower Delph Road we arrive at a junction with Church Street which has descended the bank to meet us at the hamlet of Silver End. In fact if we turned right we would start climbing the bank back to the point where *Brierley Hill: Brockmoor, Bromley & Pensnett in Old Photographs* began its survey.

Silver End consisted of houses built on the main road and along Silver Street which provided access to the Primitive Methodist chapel and to the pottery works. Bull Street was the location of a few more houses but was more useful in providing access across the railway and canal to the brickworks and iron foundry. The area on the other side of the main road fell away steeply towards the canal and was home to more small coal and fireclay pits and to brickworks that established themselves along the canal bank.

Once the main road itself crossed the railway, by Brettell Lane station, the presence of brickworks was even more prominent, and it wasn't until descending towards Hawbush that the main road became residential again.

The Primitive Methodists built their chapel in Silver Street, Silver End, in 1856. The last service was held there on 19 July 1970, although it was later used by the Mormons until faced with demolition in the early 1980s. This picture was taken in about 1980. *(Stan Hill Collection)*

This A3-sized single-page brochure was produced at the end of the nineteenth century to advertise the earthenware items produced at the Silver Street Potteries at Silver End, on the opposite side of the road to the chapel. The pottery seems to have been established in 1820 and John Jeavons took it over from Thomas Meese. After it closed the premises were used by Francis Lane, but no trace remains today. John had three sons: John, Harry and Tom. They sold pottery in the early 1900s and John became tenant of the Birch Tree pub on Amblecote Road. Harry became licensee of the Crown, Brettell Lane (see page 106). John Jeavons Snr was the great-grandfather of Mary Smallman, seen on page 38 of *Brierley Hill: Brockmoor, Bromley & Pensnett in Old Photographs. (Mary Yates)*

The last Sunday School photographed outside Silver End chapel in July 1970, accompanied by Mrs Kate Dublin and the Revd Mr Hawthorne. *(Margaret Gallier/Stan Hill Collection)*

R.M. and R.E. Evans stand outside their shop and post office in Silver End, next door to the Vine public house in the 1970s. The post office closed in December 2008. This little parade formed the centre of Silver End – at the top of Brettell Lane. *(John James)*

Above: A Coronation party of June 1953 assembles outside the Vine at Silver End. On the left is Mrs Elsie Hill, on the right are Mrs Grainger and Mrs Allen. The pub had an attractive tiled frontage of 1930s vintage but not even topless barmaids could save it in recent times and the premises have now been much rebuilt. *(Bob Hill)*

Left: Joe Smart, born in 1910, stands in the doorway of the original post office in Silver End just after the First World War. It was run by his sister Lydia Hadley, née Smart. Joe attended Bent Street School and ran to Silver End each lunchtime to act as paperboy for his sister. Lydia had joined the post office during the First World War and was rewarded afterwards by being allocated this sub post office. *(Gloria Smith)*

Malcolm Cartwright, Tony Williams and Alan Hill stand by the street sign in Bull Street. Behind them are the homes of Mr and Mrs Howarth (24) and Mr and Mrs Hill (22). The Hill family left this house in 1964, after which it was demolished. To the left of no. 24 we can see the course of Bull Lane which led to the footbridge over the railway by Kingswinford Junction. At one time there were more small houses in Bull Lane and a coal yard operated by Mr and Mrs Jewess. (Bob Hill)

Jack Hill's new Ford Popular is parked outside no. 22 Bull Street, but the photograph also shows us the view across Bull Street towards George King Harrison's brickyard on the far side of the railway. In the background we can just make out the hazy outline of the offices of Brierley Hill foundry (Messrs Bailey & Pegg) beyond the parapet of the railway bridge. Bull Street today also provides access to the Springfield Road Estate and to Addison Road which skirts Hawbush to head for Farmers Bridge on Moor Lane (see *Brierley Hill: Brockmoor, Bromley & Pensnett in Old Photographs*, page 26). (Bob Hill)

One of the pleasures of the 1980s was to be able to stand on footbridge at the end of Bull Lane at Silver End and watch trains coming and going at Kingswinford Junction South signal-box. On 14 September 1983, no. 45074 had just come off the Pensnett branch, and pauses by the box. On 14 November 2001 arsonists destroyed this box – a feature of the Silver End landscape for eighty-five years. It had been built during the First World War in anticipation of greater traffic at the Moor Street Yard, and the upgrading of the branch, known originally as the Kingswinford branch. *(Ned Williams)*

Class 45 diesel locomotive no. 45034 comes off the branch to Pensnett (the line that once headed towards Wolverhampton, via Wombourne) on 18 July 1985 at Kingswinford Junction by the south signal-box. Behind the train we can see the Moor Street goods yard and the main line heading towards Round Oak. The Moor Lane bridge can be seen in the distance. *(Paul Dorney)*

Kingswinford Junction South signal-box also controlled access to the goods yard north of the junction. By the 1970s this had become the Brierley Hill Steel Terminal and here we see coiled steel being unloaded at that time. The yard went through several uses, openings and closures, closing altogether in 1993. Road access was from Moor Lane. *(Author's Collection)*

Bull Street, Silver End, also crossed the railway close to Kingswinford Junction, and provided access to the Brierley Hill Iron Foundry. It also provided access to the Springfield Estate, totally surrounded by railway and canal. The Springfield Stores, Springfield Road, photographed here in October 1985, served this isolated estate. *(NW)*

Just before the junction with Springfield Road, Bull Street divided, one street leading past the Brierley Iron Foundry to what became Addison Road, and the other descending past the back of the Harrison Pearson Firebrick Works and over the canal into the Hawbush area. The point where Bull Street divided was watched over by the Bulls Head, the home of Black Country Ales for the past few years. *(NW)*

Addison Road was developed between the wars and became home to Brierley Hill Cemetery. In 1928 the Dudley Co-operative Society opened a new branch in this grand purpose-built building (another Jennings erection), now trading as Dhaliwal Stores. Candle Fat Alley runs between Addison Road and the canal, reminding us that the Lowther Brothers made miners' candles in Addison Road many years ago. *(NW)*

Back on the main road, in about 1935 Joseph Green Snr bought the house just visible on the extreme right of this picture, and purchased the adjoining land to build a garage for his growing coaching and haulage business. In later years a petrol station occupied the forecourt and Midland Counties Dairy built a depot to the left of this scene.

Joseph Green started his working life as engine driver at Plant's Hollow pit but by the age of twenty-four, when he married Florence, he had started a haulage business with one lorry, and ran a smallholding near Plants Hollow. The lorry was also used to convey local girls to and from the Kidderminster carpet factories. By the time the Greens reached the Silver End site seen at the top of the page, they had lived in Moor Lane and Addison Road and had run several other enterprises. Joe Green won a contract for providing transport to and from the Austin factory during the Second World War and bought old double-deckers such as these for the purpose. (Jenkins' Bakery and Larkham's fish and chip shop are visible across the road!) Joseph died in 1956 but by then his sons, Stan and Joe, had moved into the totally new business of running coach tours to Europe. This had started in April 1953 by taking some Tipton schoolgirls to Paris. Joe and Stan expanded the business, opened an office in the High Street, and returned to haulage. Green's Continental tours, direct from Brierley Hill to Europe, became a great success but circumstances changed and the company closed down in 1988.

The Green family pose with their Chrysler car beside the garage just after the Second World War. Left to right are Frances Green, Joseph's mother who had helped out when they ran a small coal business in Moor Lane; Florence Green who had worked as conductress on the buses to the Austin factory during the conflict; Joseph Green; and his son Stan who had returned from the war with ambitions, shared by his brother Joe, of building up the coaching business. *(Joe Green Collection)*

One of Greens' first coaches to be used on the Continental tours was CVD 670, a Leyalnd PS1 with a Park Royal body. It is seen here in the yard at Silver End in the 1950s. *(Joe Green Collection)*

In the early days Joe Green's coaches carried a Vine Garage fleet name as the garage was named after the pub on the opposite side of the road. The Green family also owned the house next door – both garage building and house survive although the business is no longer a feature of Silver End's landscape. *(Joe Green Collection)*

Way behind Joe Green's garage the Stourbridge Canal was winding its way to The Delph where it would make an end-to-end connection with the Dudley Canal. The Silver End side of the canal had been industrialised with a bottle works, a boiler works and another iron works but the other side of the canal was a wilderness of collieries and fireclay mines. Here, just before the Seven Dwellings Bridge, we see the Crown Wharf where a tramway terminated from the Crown Works of E.J. & J. Pearson, and bricks could be loaded into canal boats. *(MPLHG)*

Between the Crown Wharf and the railway bridge just south of Brettell Lane station was another extensive brickyard wharf of the Clattershall Works – squeezed between the northern bank of the canal and Meeting Street. This works was also owned by Messrs Harris & Pearson, whose headquarters are illustrated on page 107. The kilns seen behind the wharf lasted until the 1960s, but the area is now an industrial estate. *(MPLHG)*

The King's Arms in Brettell Lane at Silver End. The Webb family kept the pub from about 1845 to 1870 and it was then run by James Brace Rhodes. It was only kept by William B. Wood – as seen in this photograph – for a short period at the beginning of the First World War. It seems to have closed in 1921. *(Ron and Madge Workman)*

The Crown was well below pavement level and originally had a flying staircase to the entrance on the upper floor. Harry Jeavons, the landlord, is seen at the entrance in about 1910. His father, John Jeavons, had owned the Silver End pottery works. *(Mary Smallman)*

Just beyond the Crown is the Harris & Pearson building – originally built as the company's offices in 1888. The building was restored by the West Midlands Historic Buildings Trust in 2004/5 and looks superb topped by its rooftop lettering. The company had a large brickworks just behind this office which was last used by the Dyson Group plc in 1990. Silver End is in the centre of the firebrick industry and a number of companies have been working in the immediate area. *(NW)*

From Samuel Taylor's Chain and Anchor Works, seen in the right-hand foreground, the canal turned right and headed for the bridge under Brettell Lane. Looking straight ahead we see the bridge over the entrance to the basin serving George King Harrison's Brettell Lane firebrick works. This was the location of a major subsidence in November 1903 in which the canal drained and the area flooded. *(MPLHG)*

Mrs Ellen Coleman of York Avenue, Hawbush, was known as 'Nellie the Brick Lady' – at eighty-three she was still working at Price Pearson's yard when this picture was taken in 1969. She had worked there for sixty-seven years and was making 250 firebricks a day. The brickyards had a tradition of long service and widespread use of female labour. More pictures of E.J. & J. Pearson's yard in The Delph appear in *Quarry Bank & The Delph in Old Photographs* pages 98–103. *(Stan Hill Collection)*

The Foley Arms became well known because it was bought by Joseph Paskin Simpkiss in 1921 and he developed the brewery on the site. It was enlarged in 1934 by his son Dennis Simpkiss, and in 1985 Dennis's son, Jonathan, sold it to Greenall Whitley who demolished it. However, the pub itself has survived although it is now called the New Wellington. *(Stan Hill Collection)*

Class 51xx 2–6–2T no. 4140 steams into Brettell Lane station on 21 July 1962 with an early afternoon northbound stopping train only a fortnight before passenger trains were withdrawn. The ancient wooden buildings and footbridge would soon disappear and today there is very little evidence of the station, although freight trains to Round Oak still pass through this location. *(Ron Hartshorne)*

Looking back along the Stourbridge Canal with the Chapel Street flats on the skyline. Buildings which were once part of the canalside brickworks along this stretch of the waterway have now found new use. For example, here we find Delph Marine in February 2008, by then only repairing boats, but boats had been built by the company – the last was *Vindy IV*. *(John James)*

Hawbush Primary School began life in 1930 as two separate schools – an infants school and a junior school – which stretched out in a great line along Hawbush Road. It was built in the style that was popular at the time with long corridors that were open to the elements – similar to the schools built in Pensnett and Quarry Bank and the girls' school at Brockmoor. In the 1970s the 'campus' consisted of a first school and middle school, but these were amalgamated and physically joined to create the present school in 1983. A community room was a later addition. Banks at either end of the ground seen in the foreground once concealed air-raid shelters. *(School Archive)*

The view at the other end of the complex reveals the nursery school building which was added in the 1970s. *(School Archive)*

This picture only gives a slight impression of the extent to which the classrooms and halls of the Hawbush schools stretched along their lengthy corridors which were walled-in at some stage. The two halves of the building mirrored one another although it is assumed that the junior school was the larger. At the time of the 1983 amalgamation staff insisted that these corridors were linked and the space between the two halves of the complex was filled in, leading to changes to the main entrance to the building. Major alterations started in 2010.

Miss Perry (now Mrs Edwards), with her Year 2 class in 1986 on the outside of the corridor. *(School Archives)*

Above and below: Hawbush Junior School footballers of 1950/51 and, below, Hawbush netball team of 1954/55. The school was built to serve the large estates that began to fill this part of Brierley Hill from the 1920s onwards: Springfield, Hawbush and later Swanfield. Some families have stayed in the area for three or more generations – all of which have passed through the schools – and many staff have put in long service.

A recorder group at Hawbush in 1979. Left to right are Sara Hadley, Nicholas Bryan, Tracy Nock, Vicky Abbott and Dawn Gill. Thirty years later the school still has some rooms with painted bare brick walls and signs of ancient heating systems alongside modern features like digital interactive whiteboards. Some ceilings have been lowered and some rooms have been divided, but the environment is about to change again to meet the needs of Hawbush in the twenty-first century.

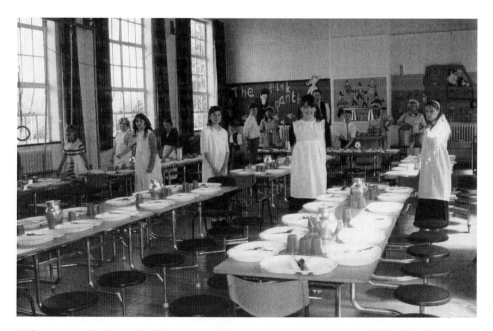

Girls pose in the dining hall in nineteenth-century costume during 1990 while the school was celebrating its sixtieth birthday. Modern fold-away tables in the foreground contrast nicely with the sixty-year-old windows and radiators in the background. *(School Archives)*

The staff of Hawbush Junior School in about 1970, before becoming a 'middle school'. The headmaster, seated in the centre, was Mr Chittock, and behind him is his deputy Mr Baker. *(School Archives)*

Above and left: Headteacher Mrs Riley with a child from Year 6 and a child from Year 1 preparing to cut the diamond anniversary cake when Hawbush Primary School celebrated its sixtieth birthday in 1990. The following year, on 18 September 1991, the Mayor of Dudley, Councillor Geoff Tromans, opened a new community room at the school. *(Janet Parkes Collection)*

Many children growing up in Hawbush enjoyed holidays provided by the school. Here we see pupils departing for a trip to the Isle of Wight in the mid-1980s in a smart green and white Leyland Tiger coach provided by Green's Tours (see page 103). *(Janet Parkes)*

Mrs Jo Horton (née Welch) and class 6A of 1991. Mrs Horton still teaches at the school today. Other staff with long service have inlcuded Mrs Hopkins who superintended the amalgamation of 1983, and Mrs Parkes who taught at the school from 1958 until 1994 and is now the chair of governors.

Having decided that the church in The Delph had no future, the parish decided to press ahead with the construction of a church on the Hawbush estate. The foundation stone seen below the cross was laid on 10 July 1954. Thanks to financial assistance from Arthur Horton, the church was eventually built and was dedicated by the Bishop of Lichfield on 22 January 1955. On 20 June 2003 community-based learning facilities were added to the church. *(NW)*

In the centre of the acres of housing now covering the Hawbush area is the Oakfield Tavern on an imposing site looking north-westwards towards Wenlock Edge and the Wrekin. It was designed by Farmer & Farmer of Birmingham in fine 1930s 'Tudor Road House' style and was opened in 1939.

HAWBUSH AND THE RISE OF COMMUNITY CENTRES IN BRIERLEY HILL

The first community centre in Brierley Hill was the old Art College in Wordsley that was launched in the 1930s. After the war BHUDC found there were ways of funding the construction of community centres out of the housing budget and this led to the provision of centres in each of Brierley Hill's 'satellites', starting with Hawbush.

Hawbush led the way because Hawbush House and the nearby pavilion of Hawbush Tennis Club became surplus to requirements when the first phase of the Civic Centre opened in 1954. The Architects' Department moved out in 1955 and the Community Association moved in. The former then drew up plans for the new standard Brierley Hill centres and one by one they were built. Hawbush CC opened on 14 April 1964 and within a year or two was planning extensions as well as retaining the use of Hawbush House. It was a hive of activity, and the association's president was H.C. Roberts and the secretary was none other than Stan Hill. The extensions opened on 21 January 1967, aided financially by the Stourbridge Cycling Club, who were to share the facilities.

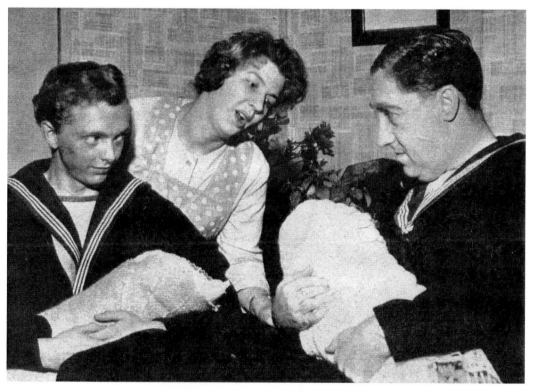

The Community Players took to the stage at the Hawbush Community Centre, presenting plays produced by Gladys Williams. Here we see the September 1967 production of *Rock-a bye Sailor* featuring John Corbett, Janet Watkins and Bob Greenwood. The next day the hall was cleared for a rabbit show! *(Stan Hill Collection)*

The range of activities undertaken in Brierley Hill's community centres is mind-boggling and Hawbush led the way with dances, youth groups, wives' groups, old people's groups, drama, and courses run by the Workers' Educational Association. In October 1967 the Brierley Hill Dog Training Club was inaugurated at Hawbush and was an immediate success. Here M. Deeley, J. Roberts, D. Ashman, J. Tromans, and G. Quinn practice giving simple commands to their dogs.

Later in the same year the 1st Brierley Hill Guides provided Christmas dinner for the local physically handicapped group. Guides Lynn Hall and Linda Grainger serve soup to Mrs Clift, Mrs Bridge and Mrs Poultney. *(Stan Hill Collection)*

9

BRIERLEY HILL FOLK

Brierley Hill has a history of being a busy sociable place with plenty of human activity centred around its churches, chapels, workplaces, political and social clubs, sporting and cultural organisations, charities, etc. Some of these were very 'local' and belonged to the communities described in these books, while others embraced the whole town. It is only possible here to provide a quick glimpse of some of the things that went on.

Brockmoorites and Bromleyites come from Brockmoor and Bromley, and Quarry Bankers come from Quarry Bank, but what do you call the chaps and wenches from Brierley Hill? Someone suggested 'Hill Billies', but few will find it a helpful suggestion! Nevertheless we could debate endlessly on the question of Brierley Hill 'identity', whether it came to exist in the past, and the question of whether it is alive and well in the twenty-first century? This kind of question concerns the Black Country as a whole and therefore what might be interesting is that alongside the intense loyalty that Black Country folk feel towards their own patch, there might be an emerging regional feeling that 'We're all in this together!' We are all living in towns built on the back of mineral exploitation and industry and we all have to find a way forward. The regeneration we are all looking forward to is complicated in Brierley Hill because the old town has to live alongside the new world represented by the Waterfront and Merry Hill – but if Brierley Hill folk find a way through all this, there will be hope for us all!

Herbert Hex, seen here leading a civic parade, was a champion of Brierley Hill. He came to the town as deputy town clerk in 1934, and after the Second World War, as town clerk was a strong advocate of the town being granted 'borough' status. *(Stan Hill Collection)*

The town's famous football team was Brierley Hill Alliance. It was formed in 1887 by the amalgamation of two Brockmoor-based teams. A football ground at the end of Cottage Street was created by levelling pit mounds and, in 1889, the club joined the Birmingham & District League. Here is the 1937/38 team consisting of Messrs Jones, Smart, Billingham, Jigger, Winwood (trainer for forty-two years), Young, Caddick, Addis, Postin, Handley, Wilkes, Tinkler and Hornby. *(Colin Storey)*

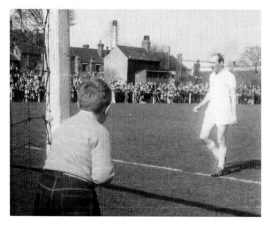 

Bernard Bresslaw makes an appearance on the Cottage Street ground in a show-business team. Note the famous floodlights! *(Colin Storey)*

These lads from Bent Street School were winners in a miniature garden competition in the late 1950s. Left and fourth from left are the Garbett brothers and second left is Reg Green. Unfortunately the cup-holder is unknown, while Colin Storey is on the right. They are standing in the playground of Bent Street School. There was no playing field at the school, and at the time the only sport played had to be rounders! *(Colin Storey)*

Pig-roasting at the 1973 Bromley Gala. Members of the Scouts' fund-raising committee make the first slices: Mr C. Bagley, Emmie Davies and Lily Porter. *(Gwen Hartill)*

Dancers line up to appear in the Brierley Hill Amateur Operatic Society's 1974 production of *Merrie England*, presented at the Civic Hall during October. Left to right are Jenny Wheeler, June Homer, Carole Martin, Dorothy Lucas, Hazel Millward and Sonia Kennard. *(BHAOS)*

The Brierley Hill Amateur Operatic Society (now Brierley Hill Musical Theatre) was founded in 1947 under the patronage of W.F. Knott, a local butcher from a family associated with Bromley and Brockmoor. After rehearsals at the Temperance Hall, their first show, *The Arcadians*, was presented at the old Town Hall at the end of 1948. *(BHAOS)*

Brierley Hill Male Voice Choir. Alf Johnson, standing in the centre, was their conductor. Brierley Hill acquired a lofty reputation for good quality choral music before the Second World War with a choir led by Stanley Adams and later Dr Campbell. *(Pearl Taylor via Stan Hill)*

Edith Jukes, Jean Hill, Phyllis Marshall and Emily Little prepare tea and cakes for the Brierley Hill Age Concern Day Centre in Cottage Street in the 1980s. The group met in a portable hut and was established in the early 1960s when a Dudley social worker named Alec Cooper began recruiting volunteers willing to help the elderly in several groups in the Brierley Hill area. *(Frank Baker Collection)*

Many people in Brierley Hill took part in social and sporting activities supported by their places of work. For example here is the Marsh & Baxter Concert Party in their Pierrot costumes taking part in a 1920s carnival. Third from left is Luther Pearson who worked for several key local employers. *(John Pearson)*

The Marsh & Baxter football team, *c.* 1962. Standing in the back row are B. Whale, E. Postin, A. Homer, A. Bishop, A. Webster, A. Hill, R. Price, A. Homer, R. Lamb, E. Read, and H. Weston. Kneeling are E. Ellis, B. Archer, R. Hill, P. Davies and F. Light. The picture was taken on the Marsh & Baxter ground with St Michael's Church in the background. *(Peter Davies Collection)*

The Marsh & Baxter footballers in front of their pavilion with some of their officials, *c.* 1964. Back row, left to right: G. Woodcock, J.G. Vesey (club secretary), J. Stock (trainer), J. Fereday (football secretary), E. Rydes (linesman), H. Wesson (trainer), E. Postin (manager) and L. Beddard (groundsman). The club ran two teams in the Birmingham & District Works Amateur Football Association League, in which they won the Mitchells & Butlers Cup and the Wellington Shield in about 1964. *(Peter Davies Collection)*

Baldwin's apprentices team of about 1962/63, with the apprentice masters, Wilf Sadler and Billy Wells. Players include Messrs Keneen, Horton, Woodcock, Bunce, Foxall, Davies and Foley. *(Peter Davies Collection)*

The Brockmoor firm of J. Hickman & Son had a football team that played successfully in the Birmingham Works League. Here they are on the Albion ground winning the Albion Shield after defeating Palethorpes 5–2 in the early 1960s.

The Brierley Hill Junior Area team of 1953 with Mr D'Arcy Jones (Mill Street) and Mr Anslow (Mount Pleasant). They are Messrs Gregg, Rides, Roberts, Finch, Southall, Bishop, Page, Perry, Edwards, Powell and Skipton. *(Alan Perry)*

Councillor David Brookes wearing the chain of office of Chairman of Brierley Hill Urban District Council in 1959. David Brookes was a grocery shop manager at Dudley Co-op's Rowley branch but was active in many aspects of the life of Brierley Hill, ranging from the British Legion to a cancer campaign. He was a governor of three schools in Pensnett and was Vice Chair of the Pensnett Old Folks Committee. He was an active member of USDAW – the shop workers' union which was strong in the local Co-op – and was in the Brierley Hill branch of the Labour Party. *(Sue Webb)*

Stan Hill wears the same chain of office in autumn 1999 in a re-creation of an event at Quarry Bank Gala in 1961, when the chain had been worn by Bill Homer. Eileen Thompson, Pat Cox and Maureen Hill wear the tiaras they had worn in 1961. Stan was elected to Brierley Hill UDC in 1952, and became chairman in 1955 at the age of twenty-six.

ACKNOWLEDGEMENTS

Many people who helped create the first of the two books about Brierley Hill need to be thanked again for helping to create this one. Space does not permit me to list them all again so I will simply add those who have come on board more recently and have specifically provided photographs and information for this book. They include: Ray Bush, Keith Hodgkins, Clarice Squires, Gloria Smith, Marlene Hickman, Vera Birch, Roy Pugh, William Cook, Stuart Perry, John Pearson, Mary Jones, Bob Mills, John Dew, Fred Bottfield, Gwen Perry, Geoff Tristram, June Price, Maureen Dean, Gerald Lowe, Graham Beckley and Margaret Gallier.

Once again we are grateful for assistance from the Archives & Local History Centre at Coseley, the editors of the *Express & Star*, and the *Black Country Bugle* – tour hosts at Mount Pleasant School – and the author's sanity is preserved by Terri Baker-Mills. Visitors are welcome at the Mount Pleasant Local History Group on Friday aftrenoons during term time, and are invited to visit the author's website at www.nedwilliams.co.uk.

Early in 1968 Messrs H.S. Pitt & Co. decided to remove the flag and flagpole from the front of their Brettell Lane premises and donated them to the 1st Brierley Hill Guide Company, based at Hawbush Community Centre. Here we see the initial unfurling ceremony at Hawbush, conducted by Captain P. Griffiths, assisted by Lt B. Morton and the Guides and their mascot.
(Stan Hill Collection)